WHEN DID I GET LIKE THIS ?

The Screamer, the Worrier,
the Dinosaur-Chicken-Nugget Buyer
& Other Mothers I Swore I'd Never Be

WHEN DID I GET LIKE THIS ?

Amy Wilson

WILLIAM MORROW
An Imprint of HarperCollins *Publishers*

Chart on page 187: From *Your Four-Year-Old* by Louise Bates Ames, Ph.D., and Frances L. Ilg, M.D., copyright © 1976 by The Gesell Institute of Child Development, Frances L. Ilg, and Louise Bates Ames. Used by permission of Dell Publishing, a division of Random House, Inc.

Pages 246, 247, and 252: Reprinted with the permission of Little Simon, an imprint of Simon & Schuster Children's Publishing Division from *But Not The Hippopotamus* by Sandra Boynton. Copyright © 1982, 1995 by Sandra Boynton.

FIRST EDITION

Designed by Joy O'Meara

Library of Congress Cataloging-in-Publication Data has been applied for.

ISBN 978-0-06-195695-9

10 11 12 13 14   OV/RRD   10 9 8 7 6 5 4 3 2 1

for David
with whom all things are possible

Contents

WHEN DID I GET LIKE THIS ?

CHAPTER ONE

When Did I Get Like This?

This morning, my six-year-old son, Connor, told me tearfully that I "always do more nicer things" for his younger brother, Seamus, than I do for him, and if that was how it was going to be in our house, he wished he had never been born. This was because I had let Seamus, and not Connor, have the highly sought privilege of waking up Daddy for the second day in a row, but jeez louise, that was only because it was Seamus's birthday. I rolled my eyes at Connor's rant, standing there in my saggy old nightgown unloading the dishwasher; but I would be lying if I said I did not also examine my guilty conscience for other acts of less-than-evenhanded treatment I had recently committed. If Connor felt that way, my conscience was whispering, it must be my fault somehow.

My two boys are on constant watch for any such slights, and every night at dinner, they measure their two glasses of watered-down apple juice against each other to ascertain whether one of them might have gotten two or three drops more. Of course one of them will have, and in my attempt to correct this affront, I will end up sending the other into doleful protest that now, *he* has less. Pouring the exact same amount of liquid—down to the microliter—into two different glasses is not a rational standard to which I should hold myself, but that doesn't mean that my kids let me off the hook. Or that I stop trying. Day after day, I do my best to achieve something that is, on its face, impossible. This, I think, is motherhood itself.

I spend a large portion of my life as a mother falling short and then feeling bad about it. In just this Pouring of the Juice moment, for example, I might wonder: *Why can't I distract them from this nightly battle? Why can't I remember to buy nontranslucent cups? And why aren't they drinking water? Am I trying to give them juvenile diabetes?* I fail each of my three children daily in myriad ways, and every time I turn on the news or open a magazine, there is a *new* way to fall short, a new recall from their toy box, a new environmental poison from which it may be already too late to safeguard them. All I can do is fret about the damage that my deficient protection of my children, my shoddy mothering, has wrought.

Before I became a mother, if I was not good at something, it did not shake my fundamental belief in my capabilities as a human being. As the oldest of six children, and twenty-five grandchildren, I always figured becoming a mother—and an excellent one at that—would be a cinch. I mean, my mother always made it look pretty easy. But now that I am myself the mother of three small children—Connor, who, at this writing, is six and a half; Seamus, who is almost five; and Maggie, who will soon be two—I have one overriding daily thought: *I suck at this.*

And I think I am right. What kind of mother feeds her

kids dinosaur chicken nuggets? *Three times a week?* What kind of mother lets hand washing after using the toilet slide, as long as it was just Number One? My kids have no problem with either of these policies; sometimes they are happiest when I am at my most half-assed. I am the one keeping a constant, running tab of all the things I am doing wrong. If I cannot immediately see how I have failed in a particular situation, I will just look harder, certain that a shortcoming is there somewhere. Around 11:30 P.M. not long ago, I found myself consumed by the *Backyardigans*-themed gift bags I was creating for my son's fourth birthday party, suddenly certain they would be deemed without merit by his thirty-five tiny guests. Kazoos, bubbles, and assorted organic fruit leathers were hardly sufficient parting gifts. What was in the bags at that other kid's party last weekend? Should I run back out to the all-night drugstore for thirty-five packs of washable markers and three dozen Super Balls?

I was halfway to the front door before I stopped and thought: *When did I get like this?* Why do I doubt my parenting abilities, day after day? Why do I suck at something my mother was so effortlessly good at, when I'm the one with a babysitter and a cleaning lady once a week and Dora on DVR? Where did the Old Me go, the one who exercised and accessorized and took a little pride? I was a Virgo, for heaven's sake, the Tracy Flick of the zodiac! Why did motherhood have me walking the edge of wackadoo?

Truthfully, I have always been "like this": a planner, a perfectionist, and extremely hard on myself. And until I became a mother—until I became someone who *would* become a mother—it actually served me pretty well. It was not until my interior leanings met the fecund, guilt-rich soil of motherhood that they burst into full flower. Once I became a mother, I was suddenly subject to a world of experts and advertisements dedicated to making me feel off-balance and unsure. I am a sucker for these messages of self-doubt. For a perfectionist like me, there is no greener and more dangerous pasture than modern motherhood, a garden in which all my neuroses have grown to rank fruition.

Today, everything from pacifiers to preschools seems to be marketed to mothers in one overarching way: this product, the ads say in one way or another, is chosen by mothers who want what is best for their children. Well, who *doesn't* want that? Honestly, what mother would aim to give her children what is merely mediocre? But that is where the hard sell begins. If you want what is best for your child—which, of course, you do, you must, if you are to be a mother at all—then you have to utilize this prenatal audio learning system, hire this parenting coach, hang these bilingual flash cards over the changing table, provide this latest essential for your children's well-being, one of which you have only just been made aware. Should you ignore this new and helpful parenting suggestion, you are in effect saying that no, you do not want what is best for your children. Good luck sleeping tonight with that on your conscience. It is easy for people who are not mothers— who are, for example, fathers—to say, "So don't listen!" But the guilt missiles are not aimed their way.

With every step we mothers take these days, we are aware that there is only one right and true path that we should fol-low, a "better" way to feed our baby, a "best" birth. But a birth isn't best unless it's vaginal and drug-free. Breastfeeding isn't *really* successful unless we do it exclusively and for a full year. (Not for one day more than a year, though; then you're a hippie freak.) Jarred baby food is unacceptable entirely—the mother who wants what is best for her children will mill it herself from local organic produce. (In a pinch, she may choose to have Cheery Organic Farm Baby overnight her their kettle-cooked, all-natural baby purees in their biodegradable packaging, swathed in a layer of dry ice. However, that's just in case of a real emergency.)

Even if a mother manages to be superlative on all these counts, there is still something new to add to her panic list every day: bisphenol A wreaking hormonal havoc in sippy cups, salmonella hiding in after-school snack cakes, lead lurking within the delicious painted exterior of Thomas the Tank Engine. The onslaught of things we are supposed to worry about is bewildering, all the more so because it is often contradictory. Caffeine causes miscarriages! (Wait, no it doesn't! (Hold on, yes it does! (Sometimes!))) When we can't be sure that anything is safe, what are we supposed to do but worry?

I'm not saying that I am a basket case all day, every day. After seven years as a mother, I have come to believe that Teddy Grahams dropped in the sandbox are still perfectly suitable for consumption. But as I watch Maggie chow them down with her filthy hands, there will be a teeny-tiny voice inside me saying: A good mother would not let her toddler eat sandy Teddy Grahams. Why, a good mother would not let her toddler eat Teddy Grahams at all. A good mother would bring blanched green beans in a citrus broth, enough for the whole sandbox to share, and she would have used her portable steam sanitizer on the communal shovel before her daughter teethed on it. There is always a way to fall short, and so there is always a corner of my brain reverberating: you are a failure.

The really sad part is that my standards have gotten progressively lower with the arrival of each child. At this point, I just want not to be horrified by how old I look every time I pass a mirror, maybe have planned what the kids are eating for dinner before 5:55 P.M., and have a house that does not look like a crime scene. Since I put in about fifteen hours of hard mothering a day, should that not be possible? Yet I find myself unable to meet even these lowest common denominators. Chaos threatens at every moment to take over our home. I flutter and hover and multitask, but the perfectly trachea-sized LEGOs multiply across the floor of the foyer while I am not looking, and Maggie finds an orange marker and colors on the new couch, and then my husband David walks in from work and dumps out the contents of his pockets onto the hall table: seventeen coins, a partially sucked Halls in a tissue, fifty-seven receipts, and a toothpick, which Seamus will immediately commandeer as a tiny sword for his microscopic Playmobil knight.

I used to have my act together. Not anymore. Our home reflects all too well my state of inner disorganization and frayed nerve endings, and I wish I could be as Zen about it as David, who does not seek to derive his self-worth from the state of our children's toy bins. David and I have been married for ten years, together for fifteen, and ours is a relatively easy, loving companionship. There's not that much to fight about: as far as parenting goes, at least, we are nearly always on the same page. But if he is a calmer parent than I, that is because we both know who will think to rummage around in the closets a week before Easter to make sure all the kids' baskets are in there somewhere. We are like almost every family we know in this respect: the mother, whether she works outside the home or not, is the repository of all child-related minutiae, and it is she who gets to be overcome with self-loathing every time some small detail is, inevitably, overlooked.

I did not think that I was going to be a neurotic mother. I thought motherhood was going to be when I finally relaxed. As the oldest in my family, I had been babysitting for free since second grade, so I felt more than ready for whatever motherhood would throw at me. I knew how to take care of kids. The freaked-out mothers were the ones who had never held a newborn before their own. That was not me. Besides, I had the most unflappable Roman Catholic mother who has ever existed, capable of handling a brood of six, spread over nineteen years, with ease and endless patience. When my mother was my age she had five children, the oldest (me) a junior in high school, and that just floors me. I feel far too young to have responsibility for a first grader, let alone someone who has a learner's permit. But my mother went about her days blissfully—or at least calmly—and if she overthought anything about my life, I never noticed it.

But my mother did not need to overthink like I do. I think. Certainly there was less to worry about then; before the advent of Purell, you had to shrug at a few germs, 'cause seriously, what else were you going to do? But it is also probably true that back then, sweating the infinitesimal stuff had not yet become synonymous with merely sufficient mothering. My mother covered her avocado refrigerator with the yellowing columns of Erma Bombeck, who served up her leftovers with a side of wry attitude and never seemed to feel particularly bad about that. My mother's primary child-care resource was a well-thumbed copy of *Dr. Spock's Baby and Child Care*, which began, "Trust yourself. You know more than you think you do." Second-guessing was not a way of life.

My mother did the best she could, but without the pressure to make her children's every waking moment an optimal learning opportunity. For mothers today, there is no such thing as an *un*-optimal moment, an instant where we might let our attention flag without ill effect. A good mother is constantly on her guard. A choosy mother will choose If, and keep all the optimal outcomes and hypothetical pitfalls for each family member on her radar screen at all times. She will be on constant, vigilant watch.

And so I almost certainly overthink everything I do for my children, from when I should get Maggie off the bottle to what Seamus should wear to school for Orange Day. In order to stop, I have to convince myself that either (1) I know what I'm doing, or (2) whatever I am fixated on is not really that important. As a mother, there are only two things of which I am ever certain: (1) I have somehow eluded detection and have been given three children for whose care I am remarkably unqualified, and (2) every decision I make for these small, helpless beings is of the utmost, life-altering importance. Nobody disputes the enormous responsibility a mother has for shaping her children's lives: I get to shape their personalities, their experiences, their very futures. Isn't that wonderful? No. It's terrifying.

I do not worry about every little thing my children eat, touch, or see. But whenever I manage not to be neurotic, I worry, in turn, that I am not being neurotic enough. Every time I turn on the TV, that blasted Your Baby Can Read! infomercial is on, and 95 percent of me can be certain it is pure bunk, while the other 5 percent worries what it will have cost my three children that their mother did not love them enough to teach them to read aloud from *The Complete Works of*

Charles Dickens as they pooped in their diapers. A mother who has her head on straight may well be able to keep up with it all, or alternatively, ignore it altogether. Maybe I am the only mother who questions herself this way. Or maybe I am the only mother bothered by her own inadequacy. If some "slacker moms" don't give their kids a home-cooked macrobiotic meal every night, it is because they do not give a hoot. I wish I were one of those mothers. I wholeheartedly wish them well.

Much has been made of the alleged "mommy wars" and how judgmental mothers are of one another. The media portrays us as living in a mom-eat-mom world, bitterly divided into breast versus bottle, stay-at-home versus working, day care versus babysitter versus attachment parenting. But I do not think it is other mothers keeping up the daily drumbeat of my maternal anxiety. And I don't really think I'm alone in feeling this way. Most of us mothers are far too wrapped up in our own guilt to judge anyone else, too certain that everyone else is doing better than we are to look askance at a neighbor's choices. We are sure other mothers are judging us because, well, they must be, when we suck so exceptionally. But we are our own worst enemies. If nearly all of us have these daily moments of doubt, these nagging fears of failure, the ones we are hardest on are ourselves.

This book is a collection of some of the times in the last seven years that I have gone over to the far side in what began as a sincere effort to be the best mother I could be. Each time, I swore that I would never again be suckered by the "Don't you want what's *best* for your children?" question. And yet, time after time, I was. Sometimes, the record will show, I may have been right to obsess. At other times, it has been distinctly counterproductive. But I learned my first lesson about being a mother while still trying desperately to become one: for me, "just relaxing" did not work. Giving it everything I had—and then some—was what worked. As a result, whenever I am not doing that for my children, I fear I am falling short. But that feeling, like a noxious gas, can easily expand to fill all space available.

I am thrilled that I am a mother. I have never felt as low as I did when I could not get pregnant with my first child, and lived with a sinking panic that I might never become a mother at all. I love my three children, and I know every day how very lucky I am to have them. I just don't want to have sinking panic about mothering them anymore. I don't need to be perfect. I don't want to be a disaster, either. Somewhere—anywhere—in the middle would be nice.

Over the last seven years of long days with little children, I have certainly had many moments of joy, calm, and peaceful reverie. This book is about the other moments. I am still too much in the thick of things to have the perspective of experience, but if there's one thing I can be sure of, it is that my children and my mothering career are still relatively young. All in all, I've gotten off easy so far. This only gives me the sneaking suspicion that I ain't seen nothing yet. But the role of mother is one I desired above all others, and so I will probably keep on being like this—trying daily to achieve the impossible, pour three glasses of juice that are exactly the same, and give each one of my children what they so richly deserve: my very best.

CHAPTER TWO

A Little Bit Pregnant

This is how I found out that after a year and a half of trying, crying, testing, and praying, after fourteen days of biting my nails since an artificial insemination, that I was really, truly, almost certainly pregnant: a message on my answering machine.

There were other clues. My period was several days late. And after buying every kind of pregnancy test the drugstore had, I also had a drawer full of double lines and plus signs and tiny digital smiley faces. Every time I went to the bathroom, I indulged in another eight-dollar test, waited for three minutes to make sure it was also positive, then stashed it in my night table drawer with all the others, amidst the hand cream and the dried-up pens.

After I collected about seven of these tests, I pulled them all out, arranged them on the unmade bed, and examined them as a group in the afternoon sunlight. Their results were increasingly and decisively positive. Weren't they? Was I imagining it? After eighteen months of fear that I would never be a mother, after everything my husband, David, and I had been through, was I wishing all these positives into existence?

No. Taken as a group, their results were undeniable. Even so, David had stopped looking at them. He said he was going to wait until I got tested at the fertility clinic; only then could we know for sure. But since it was a holiday weekend, we had waited for three days before I had finally gone for blood work at seven o'clock that morning. Now we had to wait until "end of business day" for the results. David was at work, and I was home "writing," so what was I to do but obsess? I gathered up the tests and returned them to their hiding place in the night table. Throwing them away would have been unthinkable. Until I could know for sure, they were my only comfort: a drawer full of things I had urinated on.

I went out for a walk, trying to make the minutes go faster, resisting the urge to log on to my online infertility message board for the fourth time that day. Over the last year, I had become closer to the women who posted there, like debbymom2B and wantingbabyinkansas, than to the people I knew in real life. Only these women could understand what I was going through; only these women, like me, didn't want to talk about anything else. Ever. Not even David had such singularity of focus. When I had asked the group if anyone ever heard of seven false-positive home pregnancy tests in a row, they all bubbled over with excitement, telling me "a plus is a plus :)!!!" and asking me to sprinkle them with "**baby dust**," which is infertility-chat-room-speak for sharing your good fortune. But their enthusiasm seemed premature; it wasn't official yet, and I didn't want to jinx anything. I had resolved to stay away.

I walked until it was 4:30 P.M., as in "going on 5:00," which I felt was roughly equivalent to "end of business day," which is when my doctor's office said they would call. I hadn't given the office my cell phone number. This seemed like the kind of call one needed to receive at home, alone, without the threat of disruption from a dropped call or some Starbucks espresso machine screeching in the background. But when I returned to our apartment, my answering machine was blinking. They had already called. I took a deep breath and pressed play.

"Hellothisisthefertilitycentercalling," a bored nurse's voice staccatoed at top speed. "Your bloods came back with an HCG of seventy-six point five and a progesterone level of thirteen. We will be looking for those numbers to double in the next forty-eight hours." She hung up without further ado. Clearly, she had a lot of messages to leave that afternoon. I stood there staring at the machine. "Well, what the hell does that mean?" I asked. The machine beeped twice, noncommittally.

I called my friend Heather. Heather was my one friend from the message board who had also become a friend in real life. She and I had bonded over our "unexplained" infertility, which is the particularly frustrating diagnosis you receive when you can't get pregnant and no one can tell you why. Slowly and shyly, we had made the unlikely crossover from virtual friends to real ones, and now Heather had made an even more unlikely crossover, into the land of the pregnant. She was now four months along and, as a recent graduate from the ranks of the barren, was an expert on late-afternoon calls from the fertility clinic. I played her the message over the phone. "Those are really good numbers!" Heather cooed encouragingly, like the kindergarten teacher she was. "They're high, but not *too* high."

"What happens if they're too high?" I asked. I didn't know that was something I was supposed to worry about.

"Well. That could mean multiples."

"Twins?"

". . . or more," she said.

"Well, that would be fine!" I said.

"No, of course," she said. "It's just that *really* high-order multiples can have . . . you know . . . complications. One baby is all you need."

Heather was right about that. All I needed was one. All I needed was what I had, which was hormone numbers that were moderately high, and that needed to double, in a moderately elevated sort of way, over the next two days. After all the disappointment, the tests, the waiting, this was very good news. I should have been hooting and hollering and jumping around my apartment. I should have been running down to the lobby of my building, kissing Pablo the afternoon doorman, and then dancing on top of the taxicabs on West End Avenue. I did none of these things. Why? Because the message, although it was from a trained professional, although it was the official confirmation we had been seeking, was missing two things: the words "pregnant" and "congratulations."

When David got home from work, I took his hand and led him down the hallway to my tiny office. Squished in the corner next to my desk, I played him the message and watched his angular face for a reaction. His eyes narrowed. "Play it again," he said. I did. The vein on David's forehead started to throb. "She doesn't *sound* like it's good news," he said.

"She's maintaining professional detachment," I countered.

We played the message another dozen times, parsing the nurse's words carefully. Was she not saying "congratulations" because the numbers weren't that good after all? Was she not saying "pregnant" because I really wasn't? We knew that miscarriage rates were higher for assisted pregnancies. For a fertility clinic, throwing positivity around was risky business. Maybe they were right to hedge their bets.

Finally, David said, "Ame, I gotta say, I think they're telling us not to get too excited yet." And then, although I had no more confidence than he did, I ripped him a new one. "What do you mean?" I shrieked. "Can you just be happy? This is good news what is the *matter with you!*" Then I burst into tears and locked myself in the bathroom because he was not over the moon with joy. (That, in and of itself, should have been a reassuring sign of my hormones in overload. If only we had noticed.)

What I was really upset about was that this was not how it was supposed to go. When you share this exciting news with your husband, he is supposed to be thrilled, and you are supposed to be the one who gets to tell him. Everyone knows that. Everyone's heard the adorable stories of choked-up daddies-to-be and memories that last a lifetime. Over the past several years—all my adult life, really—I had eagerly consumed what TV, magazines, and obsessedwithbabies.com had to say on this matter, and by this time I had in my head a sizable compendium of this knowledge: What to Expect When You Tell Your Husband You're Expecting.

Telling your husband he is going to be a father will be one of the happiest moments of his life—and yours! The remembrance of the look on his face, the tears in his eyes, will stay with you forever. So why not take that extra step to make this momentous announcement even more special? Try these ideas:

- Serve him baby-back ribs and baby carrots for dinner, and Baby Ruths for dessert! Then ask him if he noticed a theme . . .
- How about telling him you've left something in the oven, and leaving a little bun for him to discover?
- Ask him to fold the laundry for a change, and hide a tiny pair of baby socks in the basket!
- Take him back to where he popped the question. Hand him a bracelet box with your pregnancy test inside, and ask, "Will you be a daddy?"

This all haunted me as I sniffled to myself on the bathroom floor. I would never serve David baby-back ribs for several reasons, not the least of which was that I wouldn't begin to know how to prepare them. But I also knew that our babies—and who knew if we could even have more than one, if we could even have *this* one—would never be surprises. They would always be hard-won.

I was wrong about that. I would indeed one day tell my husband "I'm pregnant!" and watch his jaw drop and his eyes open wide. The vein on his forehead would throb in a good way. I would shock him, and I would be shocked myself. And in the end, I wouldn't do anything to amp up the announcement. I would not wait until I had ordered an I'M A BIG BROTHER! T-shirt for Connor or until I could decoupage David's bedside lamp with my ultrasound photos. In the end, I would just come out and tell him the moment he walked in from work. Even so, it is a moment I will never forget.

I wish I could go back and tell myself that day would come. I wish I could have seen then that I would sit here and write while my third baby was down the hall loudly protesting her morning nap. I could have let that moment, hovering over the answering machine with my husband, be what it was—not what I had imagined or hoped for, but something wonderful nonetheless.

Instead, there we were, with the good news we had prayed for but were too scared to celebrate, let alone share with anyone else. I was dying to tell my mother, but somehow breaking the big news with "Our human chorionic gonadotropin number is making our reproductive endocrinologist cautiously optimistic!" seemed like it would dampen some of her excitement. Both David's folks and mine had been high school sweethearts, and all of them were parents by the age of twenty-four. My mother could literally not have conceived me any sooner: I was born nine months and one day after their wedding. Not being able to get pregnant was just not part of their frame of reference. In their day, either you could have children or you couldn't. There was no gray area of surgeries, and spun sperm, and self-administered ovulation induction. Wanting and praying was supposed to be enough, and if it wasn't, you needed to accept God's will. I knew my mother thought what I was doing was not how it was supposed to be; I was supposed to get pregnant without the meddling of modern science. But from where I stood, I couldn't. Since I couldn't make her feel better about that, and she couldn't make me feel better about that, I didn't tell her anything yet. I just waited. I was getting good at it.

Three days later, I went back to the fertility clinic for more 7:00 A.M. blood work. That afternoon, I got another phone call. This time, I was waiting by the phone to receive it.

NURSE: Goodafternoonyournumberslookgood.

You will need to return in a week for another test. Haveapleasantafternoon.

Heather had coached me that when the nurse called, I should casually alert her as to the depth of my assisted reproduction knowledge. And not let her hang up.

ME: Wait. I mean—when you say the numbers look good . . . has my HCG *doubled*?
NURSE: Yes. It has.
ME: So . . . that's good?
NURSE: It is.

Pause.

ME: Is it . . . *very* good?
NURSE: We can presume that the embryo is doing well . . .

My stomach did a little flip. She said "embryo"!

NURSE: . . . but viability cannot be determined for several more weeks.

Nurse Rapidamente two, me zero. In other words: don't paint the nursery just yet.

To be realistic, I was only four and a half weeks pregnant. Since a pregnancy is aged from the first day of your last period, not from the actual day of conception, I had an embryo that was really only two and a half weeks old. Crumb sized.

Most women at this stage would have no idea they even *were* pregnant. When my mother was pregnant with me, it dawned on her that she had missed her period when she was about six weeks along. (She was still writing thank-you notes for all their wedding gifts, so maybe she was a bit distracted.) She looked up an obstetrician in the phone book, and they gave her an appointment to come in. *Two months later.* She just did her thing, and by the time her pregnancy was official, she was already wearing smock tops.

I knew it probably wasn't healthy to be aware of this potential baby as soon as its cells started dividing. It did, however, give me the opportunity to be incredibly vigilant. After spending several days reading every book at Barnes and Noble and exhausting every search engine term for protecting a nascent embryo, I understood that one truly could not be too vigilant.

> Safeguarding your pregnancy is particularly important at this vulnerable time. Shun any activity that might prevent implantation in your uterus from occurring.
>
> - No alcohol.
> - No caffeine.
> - Drink plenty of water.
> - Do not overconsume water. Too much fluid can be detrimental.
> - No exercise, except for walking.
> - No swimming. Chlorine can be toxic.
> - Avoid hair dye and nail polish because of unsafe fumes.
> - Avoid lifting, stooping, or twisting from the torso.
> - Wear loose clothing so as not to constrict the ovaries.

- If you have to travel, ensure that it will not be over bumpy roads.
- Keep social contacts to a minimum.
- Avoid standing for long periods of time.
- Avoid sitting for long periods of time.

No standing, no sitting. Got it. Wait, there was one more:

- Above all, avoid stress. It can cause a chemical reaction that may lead to miscarriage. Try to relax!

As if.

Now, honestly. If the human race were really this fragile, we would never have survived the Paleolithic Era. But I wasn't taking any chances. I reclined on the couch as much as possible, feet carefully elevated above my heart. I stopped meeting David at the door with a kiss when he came home from work, because that would have meant re-creating the exact angles of my seven throw-pillow props. I was on self-imposed couch rest, overdosing on *A Baby Story,* willing my uterine lining to thicken.

The preventive measures seemed all the more important because there were no proactive ones, nothing I could do to make the pregnancy *more* viable. You can't do headstands or drink wheatgrass tonics to make your hormone levels stay high. They either will or they won't. After everything I had gone through, this was still something I had trouble accepting: my body was independent of my will. I could freebase folic acid all day long, but in the end, it was up to my uterus, not me.

When you can do nothing except *not* do, the forbearance is all you have. Avoidance is your talisman. Abstaining from tuna salad is the only proof that something is happening. You don't look pregnant. You don't feel pregnant. You can't talk about being pregnant. I missed my friends on the message board, but I couldn't go back there now. In their eyes, I was an alumna, and it would have been unseemly to stick around. But I couldn't move to, say, the "First Trimester Friedas!" board, because I wasn't yet entitled. The next time I went for an ultrasound, I might find that the embryo had become a "blighted ovum." I would have stopped being pregnant without even knowing it.

Even the ultrasounds, after the first dozen, became less reassuring. The technician would lubricate her improbably large wand with ice-cold gel and put it inside me. Then we would both watch the gray clouds float across the screen. After a few moments, dull as dishwater for her and heart-pounding for me, the technician would mumble, "I can confirm the presence of the yolk sac," or "I can just make out the fetal pole. See?" But I couldn't see. To me, it was like looking at one of those photos of the Virgin Mary appearing in a tree or a tortilla. If I really looked hard, I could maybe kind of make out a lump of something, but to be honest, it didn't look like much of anything. I had to take their word for it.

Then my breasts started to feel sore. And I kept getting up to go to the bathroom in the middle of the night. And five days later, someone started eating a hot dog next to me on the subway, and the ketchup smell was so overwhelming I thought I was going to be sick. When I got home, I yelled down the hall to David, "Guess what! I almost vomited on the 1 train!" and he was as thrilled as I was. Nearly vomiting was nearly tangible. These symptoms could have just as easily been caused by the extremely unpleasant progesterone suppositories I was putting into service each evening. Still, the nausea was Something; and if Something was happening inside me, would it still be jinxing things if we allowed ourselves one moment of hope?

By now, it had been almost three weeks since I took the fistful of pregnancy tests that remained in my night table drawer. We still hadn't told our parents, but at this point, that seemed cruel and unusual punishment for all involved. Our parents knew nothing more than that we had undergone a "procedure," but even with that bare-bones disclosure, they would think we must have heard something by now. I pictured my mother, her mind returning to us each night as she cleared the supper dishes, afraid to ask, dying to know.

So we took the two-hour drive to Scranton that weekend, and sat David's parents, then mine, down at their kitchen tables. "So," David began to his parents. Not one for displays of vulnerability, he was suddenly shy. "So. We have news." David's mother saw the smile stealing onto his face and started jumping around her kitchen. "I knew it, I knew it! Yes! *Yes!*" she shouted. Although her enthusiasm was tempered when we actually told her our news—which was more of a "You can't tell anyone this, but we sort of kind of hope that maybe" announcement—seeing her that sure, that excited, even for a moment, made it all a little bit more real.

My parents were more measured in their reaction. After my father had told me six months earlier that if I could only relax, it would all be fine, he had learned to keep his mouth shut. He was in a foreign land. All of us were. "We'll know more soon," I promised them. "We will pray for you," my mother said. Then we just sat there, holding our breath together. Which, in the end, was all we really needed anyway. We were tired of waiting alone. And if my mother wanted to say a few novenas in the meantime, well, that certainly couldn't hurt.

If wanting and praying for a child was supposed to be enough, we had that. Surely we had that. David and I had not been overly sanguine. I had lived in a state of suspended animation for almost a month. I had not-done everything I could. And we had finally reached the day when we could know for sure: we were meeting with Dr. Simon himself.

Dr. Simon, my "RE" (that's "reproductive endocrinologist" to you), was one of the partners at our enormous fertility center practice. He had hundreds of patients, so I had seen Dr. Simon only once before, on our first visit to the clinic a few months earlier. He listened kindly as I sobbed through my patient history while David avoided eye contact, staring instead at the faces of the three gorgeous children framed on the doctor's desk. Dr. Simon flipped through my X-rays as I talked, lingering over my ob-gyn's notes, which were impenetrable as Sanskrit to me. Then he set the protocol of my care in motion through an anonymous army of blood takers and technicians and answering-machine-message leavers. I hadn't seen Dr. Simon again because it wasn't yet time. You didn't see your RE again until it was time to go to the next step—either by ramping up your course of treatment because it hadn't worked, or by confirming a pregnancy, because it had.

The clinic scheduled my appointment with Dr. Simon for the day I was six and a half weeks pregnant. By forty-four days' gestation or so, it is usually possible to see a fetus's heartbeat on an ultrasound. If it can be seen, the pregnancy can be presumed to be progressing smoothly, and the chance of miscarriage going forward drops dramatically. If it is not there, the fetus is nonviable. It is declared a "chemical pregnancy," a chimera. Never really there at all.

"How have you been?" Dr. Simon asked as he prepared the probe with gel.

"Oh, fine," I answered, eager as always to seem a good patient. I mean, where to begin?

"Lie back, please," Dr. Simon said. He put one hand on my stomach.

David held my hand. I held my breath.

We all squinted at the lava-lamp gray screen for a few moments.

"I might not be able to see anything today," Dr. Simon said, trying to sound reassuring. "If that happens, we will try again next week."

He moved the wand gently from side to side, searching. I sucked in my ribs, raising them high up into a wishbone, so that whatever Dr. Simon wanted to see could be found.

Then I saw something. A tiny blinking light, so faint I could hardly see it. At first I wasn't sure I was seeing it. But as I stared, it was there, flashing.

"What is that?" I whispered, so as not to disturb it.

Dr. Simon regarded it for a moment. "That's the baby's heartbeat," he said. "There it is. And it's strong."

He said "baby." Then he said, "Congratulations!" Then he said he was sending me back to my regular obstetrician, and we wouldn't have to come back to his office anymore. David just looked at me, too shocked to say anything, but from the tears in his eyes I understood: he too had seen, and believed. David jumped up, shaking Dr. Simon's hand vigorously, thanking him. I lay there, still transfixed by the monitor, while they exchanged collegial back-pats.

Infertility robs you of many things along the way, but the last thing it steals from you is the ability to celebrate being pregnant, if and when it actually happens. You are told not to believe too fully, to want too much. You cannot jubilate. You only, slowly, exhale.

And so I didn't want to get up from that table. I wanted to lie there all day watching my baby, my lighthouse. I still felt very far from shore. But there he was, he had been there all along, and now I could see him at last, blinking to me in Morse code: I am here.

CHAPTER THREE

Step Away from the Jumpy Castle

As soon as I found out I was definitely, totally pregnant, I planned a pilgrimage to Liz Lange on Madison Avenue, the Tiffany of over-the-belly capris. I had walked by its windows many times in the past, hiding behind my sunglasses like Holly Golightly, looking longingly through the glass at the elegant maternity mannequins in their stretch tunics. Now I had become a prime customer, and although I did not shop at pricey boutiques like this when I was *not* pregnant, in my delicate condition, I deserved the very best.

This wasn't your "Liz Lange for Target" Liz Lange. On Madison Avenue, her maternity sweaters and trousers, in cashmere and spun silk, hung two inches apart on well-spaced racks. They were sized 1, 2, and 3, rather than X and XXL. And if shopping became too taxing, comfy chairs, bottled water, and watermelon-flavored Jolly Ranchers awaited. It was the nicest store I had ever been in. Although I was eight weeks along, I felt like an impostor being there; you could not tell I was pregnant just by looking at me. But my glow, my excitement, or merely the fact that I was in there at all, was enough to give me away to the preppy young saleswoman. "What are you looking for today?" she asked.

"Um, some—clothes," I stammered, distracted by the $275 price tag on the boot-cut pants I had been admiring.

"Don't forget, Liz designs a wardrobe of basics," the salesgirl said, reading my sticker shock and laying the pants across her arm. "You'll be wearing these three or four times a week."

The salesgirl showed me to the dressing room and offered me a stuffed prosthetic belly, which she said would approximate the size I would be at five months along. I strapped it around my waist, put on the boot-cut pants, and admired my side view for several minutes. This was even better than when I stuffed washcloths in my training bra in sixth grade. I looked great pregnant! Why, I looked just like the willowy expectant models in the pictures taped alongside the mirror. I imagined wearing these pants seven months hence, out on the town, an acquaintance saying, "I can't believe you're due next month! You look amazing!"

"Thank you," I would answer, smiling humbly. "I *feel* great."

I bought the boot-cut pants and yearned for the day I would have the belly to wear them. David was taking a series of pictures of me in the same pajamas every Sunday night, a record of the miracle taking place inside me. I hiked up my shirt to show that there was almost something to see, my stomach suddenly gassy and hard each evening at bedtime. Surely it wouldn't be too much longer before the whole world could tell. We went home to visit our families the following weekend, and since I was feeling great, we shared the big news at a family cookout. "Best wishes!" Great-Uncle Toby

said, Michelob in hand. "You know, I *thought* you were putting on a little weight in the rear, there, but I didn't want to
say anything."

I had gained exactly five pounds.

Suddenly, I wasn't so sure I wanted to look pregnant after all.

Still. My pregnancy had been so hard-won, so longed
for, I was certain I would be good at it. I wasn't going to eat
everything in sight, waking David up for 2:00 A.M. Pizza Hut
runs. I maintained my regular workout schedule and added
"Aqua Mom" prenatal water aerobics once a week. My only
indulgence was an afternoon nap, from which I would wake
up flushed with estrogen. I was feeling—and looking—better
than ever. Then I walked across the park to see my obstetrician, Dr. Merman, and stood on the scale for my sixteen-week
checkup.

Dr. Merman checked the scale twice. Then he looked at
my chart, frowning. "You've gained fifteen pounds so far," he
said.

"Have I?" I said, excited, thinking that meant my body
was off to a great baby-making start.

"By now you should only have gained eight to twelve
pounds," Dr. Merman clarified. "You're gaining weight too
quickly. Time to cut out those desserts, hmm?"

Until that moment, I had never in my life been told that
I was overeating. I didn't, really, but I can't say I ever thought
much about what I put in my mouth, either. My metabolism
had outpaced my caloric intake nicely for thirty years. But
even if pregnancy was going to be different, there was no
reason to panic. I was sure that a mere modicum of will-
power was all it would take to get my body back on track,
so I skipped the packet of sugar in my morning decaf and

returned to Dr. Merman for my twenty-week checkup. He balanced the scale and this time, barely concealed a double take. "You've gained four pounds in four weeks!" he said, then gave me what was apparently his stock prescription: "Time to cut out those desserts, hmm?"

Now I was baffled. "I *have* cut out the desserts," I told Dr. Merman's receptionist, Mary, on the way out. (She was the one I could really talk to.) "I'm not eating any more than I usually do."

"Are you eating fruit?" she replied, eyebrow cocked. Well, sure I was. Fruit was good for you, right? The more, the better?

"Oh, Lord. Stop with the fruit," Mary said. "Fruit has tons of carbohydrates." But that didn't sound right at all. If I stopped eating fruit, wouldn't the baby get scurvy or something?

For a definitive answer, I was grateful to have on my bookshelf the authority on all such matters: *What to Expect When You're Expecting.* My friend Debbie had given me a well-thumbed hand-me-down copy as soon as she heard my good news. On the cover of the edition I inherited, a pregnant woman in a dowdy dress rests in her rocking chair, looking a little sleepy, perhaps from an afternoon's exertion creating a cozy nursery. This mother-to-be has put her own reading aside and looks out at the reader and right beyond, reflecting upon her impending joy. She looks far too relaxed to have actually read what is inside the book she beautifies:

> You've got only nine months of meals and snacks with which to give your baby the best possible start in life. Make every one of them count. Before you close your

*mouth on a forkful of food, consider, "Is this the best bite
I can give my baby?" If it will benefit your baby, chew
away. If it will only benefit your sweet tooth or appease
your appetite, put your fork down.*

How could I have been so selfish? Here I was, eating to
appease my appetite! Eating because I was *hungry*! If I wanted
my baby to have the "best possible start" in life I sure had a
funny way of showing it, what with those handfuls of Honey
Nut Cheerios I was sneaking after midnight. From now on, I
would follow the book's "Best Odds Diet." What this diet was
offering my future child best odds *of,* specifically, it did not
say. But what kind of glue sniffer would opt for the "So-So
Odds Diet"? Now that I knew I could do better for my baby,
there was no choice but to follow the diet's precepts:

*Bread your fish with oat bran. Add triticale to your rice
pilaf. Those who like to drink their vegetables may be
happy to know that they can occasionally count a glass
of vegetable juice cocktail toward their three-daily green
leafy and yellow vegetable allowance.*

This was going to be harder than I thought. I had never
heard of triticale, I was nauseated at the very notion of bran-
breaded fish, and I had never, in my whole life, slapped myself
on the forehead with the too-late realization that I could have
had a V8. I skipped ahead to the "Guilt-Free Cheating" section, perhaps more applicable to my lifestyle:

*We all need to give in to temptation now and then.
So once a week, help yourself to something that may*

> *not be nutritionally stellar but has some redeeming*
> *value, like frozen yogurt or a bran muffin . . . But don't*
> *cheat at all if you find that you can't stop once you get*
> *started.*

This was "guilt-free"? A bran muffin *once a week*? Even in my hormonally altered state, I could see this was taking food obsession to a new level. (To their credit, so have the book's editors; the Best Odds Diet has disappeared from the latest edition.) But back then, these dire warnings on the evils of flour haunted me. Even if I snacked on whole wheat crackers, I felt like a pregnant woman in some obnoxious ad on TV, dipping gorditas in gallons of ice cream, eating like her distended abdomen held mere lack of self-restraint rather than a rapidly growing child. If I could not be the purist who, as this book recommended, refused even a taste of birthday cake unless it were her *own birthday,* then I was a selfish mother who deserved to be fat.

Each time I had a weigh-in at Dr. Merman's I prayed Mary would be the one doing the weighing. At least she was kind enough not to announce the damage aloud. If Dr. Merman was weighing me, I would take my earrings and socks off first, so as not to add to the grotesque number he would proclaim with a click of his pen. "Time to cut out the desserts, hmm?" he would say each time, as if he never had before, as if he thought I needed only to be reminded once to stop going to the supermarket and eating my way up and down the cookie aisle in order to get my weight back on track.

Every week I gained another pound, no matter what I did. My metabolism was glacial. I pooped once every five days. My body was hanging on to everything I gave it and clamoring for more. Feed me! *Feed me!* my body would say, and I tried not to listen, even though it was *making another human being*, because my pregnancy journal said that by week twenty-seven, I should have gained eighteen to twenty-three pounds, and I had gained . . . twenty-seven. I could have chucked this pregnancy journal, or at least found one that wasn't such a buzzkill, but I felt I deserved these reminders. Four pounds over the recommended range was four pounds of weakness. If my body wouldn't listen to me, Dr. Merman, or the pregnancy journal, it might listen to the Liz Lange boot-cut pants I had longed to fill, which were now, in month seven, laughably small.

Everywhere I went my body was thoroughly scrutinized. I had thought I would revel in this attention. Instead, I felt like the prize heifer at the state fair. Friends, relatives, even strangers would have me stand in the center of a room so they could examine me from each angle and decide, based on how I was "carrying," whether it was a boy or a girl. When Aunt Marie (known for never guessing wrong) announced at my baby shower that I was having a girl, I could not share the gathered crowd's enthusiasm. I knew, according to Aunt Marie's system of divination, that her saying "girl" could only mean my ass had gotten huge back there. I have heard tell of women who delight in their Rubenesque selves. I was not one of them. "I could tell it was you coming by your waddle!" my friend said when I bumped into her on the corner, thirty-eight weeks along, and at least she enjoyed it. My baby was also enjoying itself thoroughly, bouncing around all day in the jumpy castle I had become. I was the one who couldn't wait for it to be over.

Connor arrived right on his due date, a good healthy weight, not the eleven-pound monster the pregnancy bestseller/harbinger of doom had raised as a distinct possibility for a mother as gargantuan as I. As I walked the maternity ward hallways with my baby the next day, I spotted a scale by the nurses' station. Next to Connor himself, I figured this would be the greatest payoff of childbirth: counting him, the placenta, and all the accessories, I would have lost at least fifteen pounds in the previous day's activities! But when I stepped on the scale, not only had I not lost weight—despite having unloaded eight pounds into the Isolette next to me, I weighed a pound *more* than before he came out. I'm still not sure how that is physically possible, although the four bags of IV fluid I had during my twenty-one-hour labor might have had something to do with it. Really, the very idea of scales on maternity wards seems sadistic, or at least premature.

Over the next six months, though, all the weight came off, thanks to StrollerFit, breastfeeding, and most significantly, the return of a living person's metabolism. As Connor grew, I shrank; it was as if he was sucking the fat out through my boobs and depositing it directly onto his considerable thighs. I looked great! I was back into my skinny jeans! Just in time to get pregnant again!

This time, I was digging out the Liz Lange boot-cuts as soon as the EPT was positive. There is a certain evil muscle memory that occurs in the body of a woman who has been pregnant before. "Oh, *this* again," your abs say, and surrender immediately, rather than fighting the good fight for twenty-five weeks like they did the first time around. It is considered bad luck to tell family and friends you are pregnant before your second trimester, but when strangers on the street are asking you your due date at nine weeks along, it is hard to remain coy.

I swore I would maintain a more positive mind-set about my weight this time. If I gained more than the prescribed limit, who cared? At least now I knew it could come back off again. Instead, I was filled with self-loathing as soon as my bras got too tight, because I now knew exactly how houseboaty I was about to become. Any sense of the magical when I looked at my changing body was gone.

Still, if I could have just gained my forty pounds and been left alone, I might have been all right. I will never know, because I was not. Do strangers walk up to a person who is overweight but *not* pregnant and say, "Wow, are you ever morbidly obese"? Because when you *are* pregnant, everyone feels at liberty to tell you how huge you're getting, like it's something you want to hear.

Four months into my second pregnancy, I was sitting on the recumbent bicycle, feeling rather proud of myself for having gotten my nauseous ass to the gym for once. The woman on the bike next to me leaned over with a twinkle in her eye.

"You're having a girl. Want to know how I can tell?"

"How?" I puffed, nearing the anaerobic threshold.

"Because *I* had a girl," she answered, nose crinkled with delight. "And I was all hips and thighs, just like you!"

A stronger woman might have been able to laugh this off, or better yet, *agree* with this assessment and still have the dignity to leave the house in the morning. For me, it was the beginning of an extended sabbatical in Low Self-Esteem Land. With a baby underfoot and another one within, I thought about how big I was all day but was too overwhelmed to do anything about it. I ate whatever I could find in the cabinets during Connor's nap time, and for a calisthenic regimen, I lifted him eighty thousand times a day. On this half-assed plan, I gained the exact same amount of weight as I had the first time around, when I broke a sweat daily and denied myself more than half a sandwich at lunchtime. Once my second pregnancy was behind me, I was very pissed off about this. Glad, but pissed off. When I lost all thirty-nine pounds again, I told myself that if I ever had a third baby, I was going to have a mirror on the ceiling for the birth so I could see the whole thing. But I would not look at the scale. Not even once. "Please don't share those numbers with me, Dr. Merman," I would say, smiling with a wave of my hand. "My body will do what it needs to do."

I maintained this resolution all the way up until my third pregnancy actually occurred. Then I clawed my fingernails into the ground as I was dragged back to Dr. Merman's office in the Mimi Maternity Full Support Panel Jeans I never wanted to look at again. I looked hugely pregnant immediately. I *had* to watch Dr. Merman's scale make its inexorable slide to the right. How could I not? After the Liz Lange boot-cuts split across the backside in week ten, I had to be sure I wasn't gaining *more* than a pound a week this time. I worked out furiously, taking spinning classes three times a week. Then, like Penelope at her loom, I would undo any progress I had made by going directly to the bakery across the street for a cow patty–sized scone. To my shock and dismay, the scones won.

People often told me, when I was pregnant, that I was "all baby," meaning that I carried predominantly in front of me rather than an all-over increase in girth. This is a very nice thing to say to a pregnant woman, whether or not it is actually the case, and I took great comfort in it the first time around. If I had gained forty pounds, at least I didn't look it. But by the third pregnancy, my stomach got so big so fast it looked like the baby was lying perpendicular to me, head at my spine, feet pushing my belly button improbably outward like the center pole of a circus tent. Months before I was due with Maggie, people would stare wide-eyed at me on the street, hoping my water wouldn't break right then while we were standing there waiting for the light to change. I would attempt to ignore their gaze, thinking, *Please don't say anything. PLEASE. Please allow my girth to go unacknowledged*. And then:

STRANGER: What, do you have *twins* in there?

I'd come home frothing at the mouth. David would try to remind me that these people were only attempting to be nice. And so I tried to take everything said to me in the generous spirit in which it was being offered, like when our Albanian neighbor said:

LINDITA: I think is girl? Because your face? . . . Is like-a thees.

and then puffed out her cheeks as large as they would go, or when Uncle Daniel asked David, in my presence:

UNCLE DANIEL: Did she get this big with all of them?

Wasn't that so nice of him? It was so nice I wanted to kick him with my cankles. The only thing worse than being as big as I was that summer was having all those nice people remind me of it.

Even though I looked ready to pop at twenty-two weeks,

Maggie delayed her debut for a full forty, plus another eleven days for good measure. Since Dr. Merman had assured me that she, as a third child, would probably be two weeks or so early, I expected to be done being pregnant about a month before I was. The only person more disappointed than me about that was every single other person I encountered. Each morning, I'd duck-walk the boys into school to vociferous reactions of disbelief. It was like being Norm on *Cheers,* except that my arrival was incredibly disappointing. "Ammmyy! You're still waiting?!" one parent would say. "Oh my *goodness,*" another would chime in, shaking her head with a frisson of schadenfreude. Since these were my children's friends' parents, I managed to smile and shrug. But when I passed the same group of construction workers I did every day on my walk home, and one of them called out, "Holy crap, Mama, you're enormous!" I stopped dead in my flip-flops, turned, marched back to him, and stood my ground. "That is not something pregnant women want to hear," I said, "you motherfucker." I stomped away to the hoots of his coworkers, throwing them all the parting gift of my middle finger. I was doing a public service. Maybe they'd leave the next pregnant woman alone.

It's been two years since I was last pregnant, and the nausea, sciatica, and insomnia have already become distant memories, not to mention the three childbirths. But I will never forget my dread as I exceeded each time, by four whole pounds, the twenty-five-to-thirty-five-pound recommended weight gain, how I was reminded of that at each and every doctor's visit, and all the people who let me know just how ridiculous I looked every time I thought I was actually looking reasonable for once.

Before I ever had children, if I encountered a heavily pregnant woman on an airplane, in a checkout line, on an elevator, I thought it incumbent on me to acknowledge her impending joyfulness. I would smile indulgently at the stranger's adorable stomach and say: "Congratulations! When are you due?" Now when I see a pregnant woman, the bigger she is, the more assiduous I am in leaving her the hell alone. I give her thirty seconds off from talking about her preposterous size. The mommy jumpy castle is not there for my amusement.

CHAPTER FOUR

The Mother Who Prepares

In third grade, whenever I finished my assignments before the rest of the class, my teacher, Mrs. Boyle, would send me to a desk in the back of the room set at a right angle to the others, an area called the "Independent Work Corner." There was a pack of reading comprehension cards on that desk, stacked like recipes in a box, increasing in difficulty the farther back you went. The front of each card would have a brief story, on Aborigines or what have you, offering a few paragraphs of edification. The back of the card had a list of questions on what one had just read. I loved these cards, and would plow through my times-table worksheets and Jesus-themed word searches so I could return to the Independent Work Corner and my labor of love. These cards were the *real* reason I came to third grade each morning, and I yearned for the day when I would have completed every one of the hundred-plus cards, in their dozen colored sections, up to and including Aqua.

On the early spring day I finished the last card in the box, I went up to Mrs. Boyle's desk. She sat writing with red pen in her mysterious curriculum planner while the rest of the class pored over that morning's spelling test. "Mrs. Boyle, I did it!" I whispered. "I got all the way to Aqua!" Mrs. Boyle regarded me over her glasses. "Goodness," she said. She was probably thinking, *Now what the hell am I going to do with this kid? It's only March.* I saw then that there would be no grand prize for having gotten to Aqua, no certificate, no proclamation of my name over the loudspeaker after the principal's morning announcements. It was clear to me that even Mrs. Boyle didn't give a shit. The point of getting to Aqua was simply to have gotten there. But that was more than enough for me.

The Knowledge of Having Done My Best is something deeply ingrained in me, and if there is an opportunity to set the bar for myself just a teeny bit higher than other people's, I am doubly pleased. As the birth of my first child approached, preparing and planning for this life-changing event offered just such an opportunity. I attended prenatal yoga three times weekly, practicing my squats and hip openers. Our instructor, a twentysomething woman named Willow, always rewarded us with fifteen delicious minutes at the end to recline on bolsters beneath Native American blankets and, quite possibly, fall asleep. Just in case any of us were awake, Willow would read aloud to us from the books she had been studying in her training. Though she had never gone through childbirth herself, Willow loved working with pregnant women so much she was studying to become a doula. A doula guides a woman through childbirth, though she is not a midwife: a doula is not trained to deliver babies. A mother-to-be hires a doula because, while her obstetrician may be outside smoking until the baby's head crowns, a doula remains constantly at the mother's side, offering encouragement and suggestions, helping her cope with the pain, enabling the birth that mother wants. For Willow's clients, such a birth would be, it went without saying, "natural," meaning it would occur without the numerous interventions and pain relief that accompany most modern parturitions. A doula like Willow could remind the laboring mother, even in a traditional hospital setting, that a drug-free birth was something well within her capabilities.

As we mothers-to-be lay in *shivasana*, Willow read us that day's words of encouragement:

> Birthing without drugs allows one to be fully present, fully alive. Epidurals are for women who don't know the other methods of managing their discomfort. Picture a flower blossoming, and you will find joy amidst the unpleasant sensation! Birthing can even be pleasant, for the mother who prepares.

"But I don't *want* some other stranger in the room," David said that night when I brought up the idea of hiring Willow. "*I'm* going to be your labor coach. What do we need her for?"

"You have never helped anyone give birth before," I reminded him. "A doula has."

"Look, I got it," David said. "Just tell me what I'll need to do, and I'll be ready." Well, I intended on doing just that. If David was going to be my only birth attendant besides those provided by the hospital, it was clear that we would need, at minimum, an exceedingly well-thought-out birth plan.

A birth plan is a document created by discerning parents-to-be listing all of their preferences for the impending event, everything from what drugs (if any) should be offered to who gets to cut the umbilical cord. If you trust the details of your birth to the hospital's preferences, the thinking goes, your birth experience will inevitably reflect what was most convenient and expedient for the staff, rather than what was best or most meaningful for mother and child. The extreme importance of having a birth plan was discussed extensively in the books I read, books Willow recommended in yoga class, books like *Better Birth, The Thinking Woman's Guide to a Better Birth,* and *Your Best Birth.* Many mothers probably never considered that something as quotidian as giving birth, something that one's body would, at forty weeks' gestation or so, set to doing with or without one's consent, was something one could even be "better" or "best" at. But I was a *thinking* woman. Now that I knew there was a higher possible level of achievement, a summit of childbirth performance, I was going to scale it. Why, my very possession of a birth plan would set me quite apart. I imagined the kind labor and delivery nurses nodding with approval as I handed round collated copies:

Dear Hospital Caregivers and Staff,

>*Thank you for helping our dreams come true by assisting with the birth of our first child!*
>*I would like to express the following preferences for my labor, birth, and recovery:*
>*—the option to return home and labor there, if I am less than four centimeters dilated upon arrival at the hospital*
>*—access to any and all natural ways of speeding labor: hot showers, birth ball, walking hallways*
>*—avoidance of Pitocin and other artificial means of speeding labor*

I had planned to include that I wanted David (rather than my obstetrician) to announce whether the baby was a boy or a girl, and also that the lights should be dimmed for the birth, in consideration of the newborn babe's sensitive eyes. Some of these details had to be tossed in the end, since *The Best Birth Ever* said that a multiple-page birth plan might be considered a tad excessive, and even in a nine-point font, I couldn't fit it all on one page. Some things I listed I wasn't sure I actually had a preference about, although the books told me I should. "Delay the eyedrops," I was told to write, and so I did, unsure who was getting eyedrops and why I would want them postponed, only certain that my birth experience would suffer if they were not.

> *—avoidance of episiotomy, except in case of fetal distress*
> *—avoidance of an epidural. Please do not offer me one. If I am in need of pain relief, I will ask for it.*

According to what I was hearing in prenatal yoga, epidurals were the default choice of the uninformed. If I entered the birthing room armed with my breathing techniques, a big exercise ball to bounce on, and a partner willing to massage my pressure points, I would have all the coping skills that I needed—even if I didn't have a doula. I fervently hoped this was the case. But as my belly grew, I began getting unsolicited comments from other women, sometimes even strangers on the street. "*Get the drugs,*" they'd say under their breath, and then laugh, chortling darkly, almost barking with the memory.

A few weeks before I was due, my OB, Dr. Merman, recommended a particular teacher for our childbirth preparation classes. This instructor, a tiny and spunky woman named Alice, was a labor and delivery nurse who had attended the births of hundreds of babies, though she had never given birth herself. At our first class, Alice began by asking us to go around the circle and tell the group what kind of birth we were imagining. I was first. "Well, I'm pretty sure I don't want an epidural," I began, certain this was what Alice wanted to hear. Alice offered no reaction, but the woman next to me, sporting hair extensions and a mountainous belly, snorted in disbelief. "Why?" her husband said, looking around his wife's stomach at me with some disdain. "Why wouldn't you just get the drugs?"

"Well," I hedged, looking to Alice for support, "once you have an epidural, you have to stay lying down in bed. Which is guaranteed to slow down your labor. Which will lead to other interventions. If you can stay up and moving, labor will go faster."

"That's right," Alice said. "Amy is thinking of this the right way." My colleagues, however, seemed unimpressed. They were willfully uninformed, an option I had never considered. "I'm gettin' the drugs as soon as I walk *in*," the hair-extensions woman said, flipping her locks to a smattering of applause. I decided it was probably a good idea to leave the birth plan in my purse.

I was also too shy to show my birth plan to Dr. Merman, and had brought it across town for several of what were by now weekly appointments without bringing it up. This was somewhat undermining to the birth plan itself, since its whole reason for existence was so my preferences could be clearly understood by the professional delivering my child. Finally, at thirty-eight weeks, I spoke up.

DR. MERMAN: Okay! Well, I'll see you next week,
and of course call me before then if—
ME: Actually, Dr. Merman. There is one other thing.
I've been working on a birth plan.

I could see something in Dr. Merman's face, an urge to
smile, quickly quashed.

DR. MERMAN: Ah, then. Let's have a look.

I pulled the plan out of my purse and handed it to him.
He scrutinized it.

DR. MERMAN: Mm-hmmm . . . Okay . . . I do have
one question.
ME: Yes?
DR. MERMAN: I recommend constant fetal monitoring
for all my patients. Why are you requesting that it be
limited?
ME: Well, having intermittent fetal monitoring, I
have read, would allow me to remain mobile during
labor.
DR. MERMAN: It would.

He paused for a moment.

DR. MERMAN: You may find, though, as many of
my patients do, that once you are admitted to the
hospital, you will be happy to lie down.

If I had been truly committed to natural childbirth, I would have taken this conversation as proof I needed a new doctor, one who would honor my wishes rather than pooh-pooh them. But Dr. Merman did not seem dismissive when he said this, neither rigid nor patriarchal. He seemed, merely, kind.

My contractions began the afternoon before my due date. They were mild and irregular, maybe seven minutes apart, but after just a few I understood that something was beginning. I rode the subway home holding on to the pole very carefully, since no one saw fit to give up his or her seat. This was, sadly, standard treatment for a pregnant woman on the subway, but I was surprised no one around me sensed the transformative, electric experience happening inches from their opened news-papers. Whatever. I didn't want to sit down anyway! I was in labor! I was going to perambulate the whole city, pausing only to let out primal yells of hip-opening power, and when David and I got to the hospital, it would be nearly time to push.

As soon as I got home, I pulled out pen and paper so David could time the contractions and confirm their veracity. Dr. Merman had given me the 4-1-1 Rule: once my contractions were four minutes apart, lasted a minute, and continued this way for one hour, active labor would have begun. "It's starting! No, wait! Now! . . . No, wait. That wasn't one, but—go! Now! Start from three seconds ago!" I'd pant, David scribbling out what he had just written and starting over. It seemed terri-bly important to have an exact record to show the admitting nurse; that, and the early December temperature, meant I did laps around our apartment rather than the neighborhood.

When I met the 4-1-1 standard an hour or two later, David alerted Dr. Merman on his cell phone. He was out to dinner with his wife. He asked to speak to me so he could gauge my status from the sound of my voice (and, probably, know whether it was safe to order dessert). "You sound like you're doing very well," Dr. Merman said. "You go to the hospital when you feel it's time."

By 11:00 P.M., I felt it was. The contractions had moved beyond moderately uncomfortable to painfully arresting. Once one began, I would stop pacing and stand rooted to the spot, trembling involuntarily. It was, I told David, what being electrocuted must feel like. "We said in the birth plan we were going to wait as long as possible," David reminded me; he had just settled in on the couch to watch *SportsCenter* while maintaining the contractions' paper trail. "I—*have*—waited as long as possible," I hissed, holding on to the dining room table for support. "I have been having contractions for six hours!" Going by the rough benchmarks Alice had given us in Lamaze class, six hours of labor meant six centimeters of dilation. Really, staying home any longer would have bordered on the irresponsible.

We struggled downstairs in the elevator and out to the cab, David, me, and our three overflowing bags of supplies, which had been packed and waiting by the front door for weeks: comfy pillows (for both of us), robe and slippers, pajamas (for both of us), heating pad, massagers, Gatorade (no hospital-issued ice chips for me), a wide range of CD and snack selections, a "My Brest Friend" breastfeeding pillow, a homecoming outfit for the baby in gender-neutral pale yellow, and several copies of my birth plan. David had committed our plan fully to memory, under my rather extreme exhortations to do so, but I wanted it all in writing in case we were challenged on some point. I was going to have other matters on which to focus.

Once at the hospital, David filled out my paperwork while

I pushed, huffing, against the admitting desk. Perhaps I was managing my labor a little *too* successfully, because no one on the overnight skeleton crew in Labor and Delivery seemed in much of a hurry to examine me. I was finally shown to a converted closet bisected by a curtain. The examining resident, David, and I could fit in there, but our bags could not. "Let's see what we have!" the resident said cheerily, and I was grateful someone was showing some enthusiasm as I struggled onto the table. I watched her face as she examined me, her eyes darting, settling on the right number. "Great job!" she said. "You're about one and a half centimeters dilated!"

I could tell she was rounding up, throwing that "and a half" in for my benefit. "*What?*" I shrieked. "I have been having contractions for seven hours!"

"Wow! Good for you!" she said, beaming like Miss Tennessee.

"But the Lamaze teacher promised me a centimeter an hour," I said, hoping for a recount.

"Every birth is different," she said, winking at David. I saw precious little to wink about. "Now. You can stay here, if you want . . ."

I knew what she would offer next: a Demerol drip to take the edge off and let me sleep until I was dilated enough to get an epidural. This was exactly what the birth books had told me to avoid at all costs. Once I accepted any pain medication, I would be on a greased-pig slide to Intervention Town. How lovely that suddenly sounded.

"No," David said quite assertively on my behalf. "She's less than four centimeters, and we're going home. That's what's in our birth plan." Back down the elevators we went, David, me, and our three bags. I held on to the pole at the hospital entrance, finishing out another contraction while David hailed another cab. I couldn't believe that I was one of *those* first-time mothers, the ones who rush to the hospital only to find out their perceived labor pains are "false." I had thought being more prepared than other women meant I would be better able to handle the pain. Now here I was, the idiot being patted on the head and sent home because I was, more likely than not, not really in labor at all. If these were "false" contractions, I was terrified of how much worse they could, apparently, get.

The cabdriver regarded me in the rearview mirror with considerable trepidation. Dr. Merman had been right: more than anything, I wanted to lie down and be done going anywhere until this was all over with. Instead, I was in a cab speeding across Central Park at 1:00 A.M., holding on to the leather straps that hung from above the door. (I always wondered what those were for.) Every few minutes, back into the electric chair of contractions I would go. I would sit up as tall as I could, hiking up my shoulders and ribs, trying to climb out of my body, taking deep breaths until it passed. The books had said that the peaking aspect of contractions would be comforting. I found it terrifying. *Ow ow ow OW! Oh my God it's getting WORSE OW OW—is it almost—no! Ow! OW! Jesus Christ, OW!* I couldn't even enjoy the time off in between, since I knew each second of rest only brought me closer to the next ruthless onset. "I'm okay," I told David, trying to smile, and he smiled back, clearly freaking out. I was being this much of a baby and we weren't even admitted yet? He rubbed my back. "Don't *touch* me!" I yelled. (The partner massage techniques Willow had taught us at prenatal yoga would prove less than useful.)

Once home, I climbed into our bathtub. According to my birth plan, at least, this is what I wanted to happen next. David said, "Try to get some rest, hon," and immediately passed out in our bed, abandoning me as surely as Peter did our Lord and Savior in the Garden of Gethsemane. (Some doula he was.) I lay in the tub for a few hours, slumped over the side as the water grew cold, alternating 180 seconds of sleep with 60 seconds of gripping the faucet and moaning gutturally. Around 4:00 A.M., I heard a distinct popping sound, a champagne cork flying loose. It was my water breaking, though I could not be sure of that until I got out of the bathtub, toweled off, then was abruptly wet again. I went over to the bed and shook David awake. "You're doing so great, honey. Try to rest," he said sleepily, patting the pillow beside him. "Get *up*," I said, hitting him, knowing that the clock was ticking. Now that my amniotic sac was broken, the baby was going to have to come out, one way or another, in the next twenty-four hours. The hospital would have to admit me now, and I desperately desired the finish line of the birthing bed and its scratchy sheets.

After I was reexamined and told that eleven hours of overnight labor had brought me to *four* centimeters' dilation, I made the executive decision that I had labored drug-free for long enough. "Amy would like a 'walking epidural,'" David reminded the anesthesiologist, who was searching for the correct injection spot on my spine. "There is *no such thing*," the anesthesiologist responded, clearly for the eighteenth time that morning. "I can give her a lower dose, but from now on, she's going to be in bed." These were the kindest words anyone had said yet.

The epidural probably slowed my labor somewhat. It's

hard to say, since it could not really have gotten much slower. But now I was at least able to sleep through a few hours of contractions, awakened finally by the tremors of my body "in transition" but not by the pain itself. Dr. Merman arrived and pronounced me ready to push, a mere nineteen hours after my first contraction. "In accordance with our birth plan, Amy would like the epidural turned off now, so she can feel to push," David announced. I grabbed his arm and told him, in no uncertain terms, where he could shove the birth plan. The epidural drip stayed where it was.

Two strenuous hours of pushing later, the baby's head was crowning. There was an almost eerie calm in the room as Dr. Merman, the nurse, David, and I all waited there on the edge of bringing a child into the world. There was nothing for us to do but wait for my body to begin its next contraction and finish its task. It was a strange little moment, an anticlimax before my life changed forever. Dr. Merman decided to make a little speech while we were waiting. "I know you didn't want an episiotomy," he said, holding up the scissors. "But this baby's head will come out much more easily if I make a little cut."

"Go ahead," I said, waving him off, feeling nothing as he snipped, no longer focused on anything but being done. And after that next push, my son Connor was born. As our birth plan requested, he was placed immediately on my chest, sans eyedrops or sponge bath, umbilical cord still pulsing. The books had considered this point nonnegotiable, and I now saw why. My baby was with me at last, and I didn't care if he was cleaned off and bundled up or not. There was nothing my baby needed in those first moments of life but his mother's sweaty and exhausted arms. It was a perfect moment.

Well, almost. Our three enormous bags of supplies had sat in the corner, unused. I never got around to utilizing the tennis balls in the small of my back, or the guided visualizations, or the anthemic U2 music David had chosen for me to labor by. I was happy I had packed my favorite pillow, but the rest of my careful planning had gone by the wayside, including the birth plan itself.

I thought that all I had to do to have a perfect birth was state that that was what I wanted. Anything left to chance, and I would become another victim of a needlessly meddling medical establishment. But in the end, that's what happened anyway. I had an episiotomy, which the books warned me would happen to any mother who didn't stand up for herself, who wasn't informed enough to know episiotomies were performed purely for the doctor's convenience. I had known this and still not stood my ground. I had also had an epidural, which the books warned were foisted on all laboring mothers, making them woozy, disconnected, and not present in their own bodies for the moment of birth. In actuality, it had made me calm, and unfrightened, and perfectly present, except for the corner of my brain that was clanging: *You have failed.* I was holding Connor in my arms, and there was a tiny part of me thinking not of how I had made it through a twenty-hour labor to deliver a perfect baby boy, but of how I had fallen short. I was a quitter. I had not made it all the way to Aqua.

But lying there holding my son, I could also see that it was screwed up to regard my caregivers' attempts to alleviate the pain and inertia of a *primigravida,* a first labor, as the machinations of the enemy. They had only been trying to make me feel more comfortable, trying to deliver my baby to me as soon as possible, as safely as possible. And they had. That could not have been wrong.

Four years and ten months later, I was back in the same hospital to give birth to Maggie. Since she will likely be my last child, her birth seemed as momentous as my first: the final chance to do things right. After waiting eleven days past her due date, I showed up at the hospital early one morning with irregular contractions, again not really in labor. This time, though, Dr. Merman told the nurses to kick-start my contractions with an IV drip of Pitocin, the unholy crack cocaine of birthing interventions. I welcomed it readily. The nurses' shift change occurred at 8:00 A.M., and at 8:10 A.M., my new nurse, the one who would be my guide for this one last trip, walked in. "Hi, I'm Alice," my old Lamaze teacher said, and then did a double take, recognizing my last name on my chart. To have Alice as my labor and delivery nurse seemed like incredible luck, and a sign. Maybe I could tough this last birth out without the epidural. Maybe I could do it right this time, although the Pitocin would make the contractions even more painful. Maybe I could do it, because this time, I would have Alice to help. "You're laboring very well," Alice said, patting my back, bringing me a birthing ball to squat on while David went looking for a turkey burger. I was actually feeling pretty good. When Alice did the next internal exam, an hour later, I was already at five centimeters. She looked at me. "If you're going to have an epidural, Amy," Alice said, "it's time."

I looked at her, unsure. "I feel okay," I said. "And a third baby is going to go pretty fast, right? Maybe I can make it without."

She shrugged.

"What do you think?" I asked. I wanted so desperately to please her.

"I think," Alice said, "that you don't have to impress me." I gratefully accepted the anesthesia and another pain-free birth, relieved that Alice was not going to think less of me for it, even if I did.

I am not sorry that, entering into the terrifying and mysterious experience that is childbirth, the books I read armed me with information and awareness. I am sorry I created a hierarchy of outcomes that didn't matter a whit but took even a moment of happiness away from the birth of my children. The only thing wrong with Connor's birth was that *I* thought there was something wrong with it. In the hands of a perfectionist like me, the birth plan was the snake in the garden, dangling the apple of an idea that there could be a "better" or a "best" birth, one that could in any way exceed the happy ending of a healthy baby, safe in its mother's arms, both of them whole.

CHAPTER FIVE

Nipple Confusion

Despite my overplanning for the birth of my first child, the pains of labor were not the chief focus of my third-trimester anxiety. I was at least fairly certain that one way or another, in the manner I had envisioned or otherwise, my baby would be born. The primary obsession that stayed with me throughout my nesting-instinct-fueled days, that accompanied me through all my nights of parturient insomnia, was the unnerving thought that once my child was born, I was supposed to put my boob in its mouth and milk would come out.

I could easily imagine my imminent life as a mother. I just couldn't imagine *that*. I was apprehensive on two counts. Would my lactating breasts mean sudden and perhaps permanent desexualization, in my own eyes and those of my husband? At the same time, wouldn't there be something inappropriately hypersexual about my baby (particularly if it were a boy) with my boob in his mouth all the time? To me, nursing a baby was *way* out there, going off the grid, packing the covered wagon and venturing into undiscovered territory.

Like the majority of my peers, I had not been breastfed; I may have been a '70s baby, but that hippie stuff did not fly in Scranton, Pennsylvania. Out of my huge extended family, only my Aunt Nessie nursed her children—not that she ever did it where the rest of the family could see her. One of my earliest memories is of walking into a bedroom at Nana's house and discovering Aunt Nessie sitting in a rocking chair with my new cousin, Erin. It looked to me like both of them were asleep, but Aunt Nessie had her shirt off, and the baby's little chin was moving, and they seemed *connected* somehow. Aunt Nessie looked up and must have seen the confusion in my five-year-old eyes. "It's okay, honey," she said, but I was already backing out and closing the door. I didn't know what the heck she and my cousin were doing, only that I was not supposed to have seen it.

A quarter of a century later I did not have much more of a clue. I had no close friends who had already had children, no older sisters to light the path. I might as well have asked my mother for tips on ice fishing. Is there anything into which a modern woman is thrown with less support or guidance? Before getting married, my church required a weekend-long retreat of lectures and reflection. Before labor, my obstetrician prescribed fourteen hours of Lamaze classes so I could acquire breathing exercises I would immediately jettison when the time arrived. I have even attended a mandatory two-hour seminar at my children's school on how to be a parent of a child in pre-K, for the last three Septembers in a row. But there were no breastfeeding symposiums for pregnant mothers. I didn't know where to look for reassurance or advice. I watched *A Baby Story* on TLC twice daily, so I knew what would happen if the umbilical cord was around my baby's neck during delivery, if meconium was detected in the amniotic fluid. What I didn't know was how to do what was supposed to happen next.

In spite of my extreme apprehension, I never considered just not doing it. I had to breastfeed my baby, because I was going to be the best mother I could be, and on this particular point the world is rather unbudging. These days, one would have to be part of the last undiscovered tribe in the Amazon rain forest to not have heard that "Breast is Best." The rest of us have all had pounded into our frontal lobes by the Internet, by Dr. Sears, by Baby Whatever magazine, and by strangers on elevators, that breast is best! for a baby's immune system, his bonding with his mother, his IQ, and his emotional development. Formula is totally fine too, all these sources tell us, for mothers who don't really love their children. The message was fairly clear. If I was afraid of what it would be like to nurse my child, I could not stomach who I would apparently be if I did not.

My friend Heather, who had graduated from the "Trying to Conceive" Internet message boards shortly before me, had just given birth to her son, Owen. I waited about a week before I went over to visit; my mother had always told me it took at least that long before new mothers were ready for visitors. I knew Heather had planned to nurse Owen, and I hoped to get the lowdown on it while I was there. Since Heather had already been a mother for a whole week, she was sure to have everything figured out.

Owen was adorable. Heather looked horrible. "Basically, I haven't slept more than half an hour since we brought him home," she said. "It's not going very well." She spoke of fevers and infections (hers), of searing pain and cracked nipples caused by Owen's faulty "latch" onto her breast. "And now it's time to feed him already," she said, sighing. "I'm sorry you have to see this."

Heather's loving husband handed her Owen, then arranged eighteen couch cushions around the two of them just so. Then he got out an elaborate system of plastic tubing, which Heather placed around her neck and down alongside her newly enormous breasts ("porn-sized," Heather called them, without the gusto one might expect). Heather explained that the tubing was a Supplemental Nursing System, ordered by the lactation consultant, who had already made several $120 home visits (not covered by their health insurance) to help Heather's nursing go more smoothly. While Heather nursed her son, breast milk that she had pumped earlier would go through these little tubes and into his mouth, augmenting what Heather's breasts were providing. Heather would feed Owen this way for up to forty minutes, then pump more milk out of her breasts for another thirty minutes, then have perhaps an hour off before the entire rigmarole began again.

Owen fussed and sputtered. Heather looked like she was about to cry. "Open your mouth, little guy," she pleaded. I left soon after, since poor Heather was too distracted for visitors. All my breastfeeding questions were still unanswered, including a new one, more burning than all the others: if it were really that impossible, why didn't she just *stop*? Witnessing Heather's experience only served to further freak me out. Not only was breastfeeding altogether ooky, but it also seemed that it sucked, literally and otherwise.

A month or so later, David and I went to see our new baby niece, Alexandra, in the hospital. We had to wait in the hallway for at least half an hour when we got there because the nurse was trying to teach David's sister Nikki how to nurse the baby. I could tell by the look on Nikki's face when we finally saw them that it had not gone particularly well. By the next time we saw our niece a few weeks later, though, Nikki was off the hook, having been given a hall pass by Alexandra's pediatrician stating that Nikki was not producing enough milk. No Supplemental Nursing System for Nikki. She seemed pretty happy to have been sprung, as did Alexandra, who was lying there sucking contentedly on her bottle. That night, I made a pact with David: I would give nursing a try, but I was no martyr. When the first bad thing happened, I was out.

As my labor progressed, and the moment when I would meet my child neared, my anxiety increased. From my exhaustive research, I knew that babies have a strange window of heightened alertness as soon as they are born; they regard their new surroundings with serious eyes for an hour or so, then fall into the deepest of slumbers for about a week. I was certain that breastfeeding for me would be ultimately unsuccessful, but if it were even to begin, I had to nurse Connor during this narrow window of opportunity, in the first minutes of his life.

It was just as the books had said: when newborn Connor was handed to me, still covered in vernix, his eyes were wide open, regarding his new world with great gravitas. After crying over the miracle of his existence for a few minutes, I extricated myself from one sleeve of my hospital nightgown and, with my shoulders hiked up to my ears in anticipation of agonizing pain, put Connor right up to my breast, nose to nipple. He stared at it unemotionally. "Tickle his lips with your nipple," the nurse said encouragingly. I did so, with faint distaste. Connor opened his mouth, and—he was there! He was doing it! And while it didn't really seem like anything was coming *out,* it didn't really hurt, either. It felt fluttery. Kind of sweet.

I figured the hospital's lactation consultant would come in at some point that afternoon to tell me exactly how this would really work. But other than four ecstatic grandparents, Connor and I had no visitors, so the two of us practiced on our own all night. The next morning, on forty-five minutes' sleep or so, I showered and put my new robe on so we could attend the hospital's 10:00 A.M. breastfeeding class. The other new mothers and I shuffled in holding our precious bundles, settling in on our hospital-issued inflatable donuts. Our babies slept. We smiled shyly at one another. The nurse arrived last. She was not smiling.

"Welcome to 'Lactation an' You,'" she said, sounding like a cartoon thug, looking as if she'd sooner pistol-whip each one of us than ever have to give this speech again. "This morning, we're goin' ta look at your areolas, and yuh baby's latch, and make sure yuh all off to a good start."

We mothers all sat there, still smiling, awaiting further instruction. The nurse rolled her eyes. "Unwrap yuh babies! *Wake them!*" she barked. We all began frantically unswaddling. Once I had Connor unwrapped, the nurse pointed at him, cocking an eyebrow.

NURSE: How old's that baby?

I was proud that my infant was already being singled out for attention. She probably thought he had the alertness of at least an eight-day-old.

ME: He's nineteen hours exactly!

The nurse's face darkened.

NURSE: What are you doin'?

I stared at her dumbly.

NURSE: Wrap that baby! For the first twenty-four hours, the priority *is* . . . ?

We all stared at her dumbly.

NURSE: Warmth! *Not* hunguh! *WARMTH!*

I held Connor tightly to me, hoping that hypothermia had not already set in, and spent the rest of the twenty-minute class castigating myself for not having known the warmth thing. Idiot. The nurse observed the nursing techniques of the handful of babies old enough to survive at room temperature, then handed all of us pieces of paper certifying that we had received breastfeeding instruction and were free to go. The next morning, the hospital sent me home, with no more idea of how to feed Connor than I had had before he arrived. Every two hours or so, he would sort of nibble on me, and it felt not-horrible. But I wasn't sure if anything was coming out, even the concentrated yellowy colostrum that I had read would precede the actual milk. I considered that Connor could be starving slowly or drinking his fill, and no one had told me how I was supposed to know the difference.

I was obliged to spend the next several days finding things

out myself through endless hours of empirical research. This is what I discovered:

- If you can say "I'm not sure if my milk has come in yet," *your milk has not come in yet*.
- It is best to prepare ahead of time for that moment by keeping two bags of frozen peas in your bra whenever you are not nursing your child.
- When you wake up with two hot, F-cup boulders where your breasts used to be, your milk will have arrived.
- And *that* is when it will hurt, like really hurt, like, when your baby starts crying, you may start crying too, because you so dread what is coming next.

I was furious that no one had prepared me for any of this. There was evidently a vast conspiracy of silence prohibiting anyone from telling pregnant women how hard breastfeeding would be. If we were told the whole truth, none of us would have even attempted it. This added the rage of betrayal to the soup of leaking, postpartum emotions I had become.

I was cut off even from a new mother's most obvious means of support: my baby's grandparents, who stood around our living room not knowing what to make of all this. My mother watched me struggle to latch Connor on to my engorged breast, wincing whenever I did. "You mean he *never* gets a bottle?" my mother-in-law asked, wondering how she would ever bond with her grandson. My poor father-in-law was unsure where he should look, since I was sitting around our apartment half-naked. I had no shame—I had left my dignity on the delivery room table a week earlier—and the thought of any fabric touching my nipples between feedings was more than I could bear. At least I was extra-dressed below the waist: I left the "My Brest Friend" positioning pillow Velcro'd around me at all times since I was just going to have to strap it back on soon enough anyhow. "Man overboard!" my father-in-law said, attempting a kindly joke as I hobbled to the bathroom. I didn't see anything funny about it.

It was a vast twilight of uncertainty. David's Aunt Carol came over, watched me breastfeed her new great-nephew, then asked me how many ounces he had just drunk. "I don't know," I answered. Aunt Carol blanched visibly: "What do you *mean* you don't *know*?" *My God,* I thought. *She has a point!* I had no proof, other than the occasional wet diaper, that he was getting anything to eat at all, and that meager evidence did not really allay Aunt Carol's apprehensions. Or mine. All of our relatives knew better than to come out and actually say this breastfeeding stuff was utterly cockamamie, though I would not have blamed them if they had.

Then a light dawned. I took Connor to his two-week doctor's appointment, and when they put him on the scale, he had gained a pound. A *pound*! Here was the proof I needed: my body was keeping another body alive! "Nice job, Mommy!" his pediatrician said. I strutted down the street pushing Connor's stroller home. I was a cave woman, a primal superheroine: Thor Girl, with Jugs of Power. Me make baby fat!

Not long after that, nursing started to hurt less, then not at all. My breasts stopped billowing to a frightening size every two hours. Connor no longer needed three or four agonizing attempts to latch on correctly. I could pull up my shirt and pop Connor on without even looking down at him. But I spent most of my time doing just that, meeting the gaze of his old-soul eyes as he drank, the oxytocin my body released along with the milk making both of us pleasantly sleepy. Sitting there with Connor, lit by the night-light as we rocked back and forth, had become something heavenly.

This miraculous change of events so surprised me that I brought Connor to a local breastfeeding support group. Back when I actually needed it, I had felt too overwhelmed to leave the house. Now, perhaps I could be of help, offering encouragement that it could get better to new mothers who were either struggling or ready to throw in the towel. And indeed there were a dozen frazzled-looking women there, weaving horrifying tales of chronic mastitis and of thrush, a yeast infection requiring an already-exhausted mother to boil everything she and the baby wore. The moderator of the group, a serious woman with short hair and no makeup, was not exactly warm and fuzzy, but the depth of her knowledge was reassuring. She told one weeping mother that the scale proved her pediatrician wrong: she *could* make enough milk for her baby. She made one small adjustment on another baby's positioning, and the mother's pain went away entirely. Then it was my turn.

> **ME:** Oh, I'm just here to listen. Things are really going very well for us!
> **MODERATOR:** That's great to hear. Do you have any questions?
> **ME:** Well. I guess there is one thing. I'd like to introduce a bottle of breast milk at night. How should I go about that?

An Icelandic chill came over the room. The moderator narrowed her eyes.

MODERATOR: Why?
ME: Why what?
MODERATOR: Why would you want to introduce—a *bottle*?

She fairly spit this last word. All the other mothers stared at me.

ME: Well. It's just that I have to do all the night feedings, and I thought maybe my husband could take? a? turn?

I looked to the other mothers for support. One woman in braids shook her head at me, an almost imperceptible warning.

MODERATOR: Bottles taint breast milk with bisphenol A and phthalates. Bottles cause nipple confusion.
ME: . . . Oh.
MODERATOR: Do you *want* your baby to have nipple confusion?

This question was rhetorical, of course. I was not sure what exactly "nipple confusion" might be, but I thanked my lucky stars I had attended this support group before I crippled my innocent son with a lifetime of it.

With breastfeeding, as with all things a modern mother attempts, expectations are exceedingly high. Even one bottle, a mother is told, might destroy everything she has worked so hard to attain. A mother must nurse exclusively and indefinitely, even if she has raging fevers and never sleeps, even if she has to pump incessantly and feed her infant with an eyedropper. Anything less is not good enough. And so a nursing mother who plays by these rules must bring the baby wherever she goes, or else stay home. And when the baby wants to eat, on an airplane, in church, in a mall, she must endure the censorious stares of those who think she is doing something gross. My friends who formula-fed their babies told me they felt judged every time they whipped out the Enfamil. Perhaps they were, but I felt judged whenever I dared to nurse my baby where someone might see us. When a breastfeeding mother adheres to what she has been told—that there is one correct way to feed her baby—she is then told by security guards at the food court that she cannot feed her baby that way, not unless she throws on a humiliating "Hooter Hider" first. On either side are people equally inflexible in their thinking. The mother is stuck in the middle.

I dutifully followed the instructions of the lactation consultant and breastfed Connor for a year without a bottle ever touching his lips. When my second child was four weeks old, my mother-in-law (seeing that I was ready to drop) offered to get up with baby Seamus one night and let me sleep. I was too weak to resist. To my shock, not only did Seamus sleep five hours straight after that first grandmother-administered formula, but the dreaded "nipple confusion" did not descend upon him after all. Seamus switched happily between bottle and breast for the rest of his infancy, I got to sleep five hours in a row once in a while, and I was unquestionably a better mother for it, not a worse one.

Since then, I have polled enough other mothers to believe that the legendary "nipple confusion" is somewhat like the Yeti: while many of us have heard tell, no one has ever been an eyewitness. If anyone has nipple confusion, it is the mother, who gets thrown into the deep end with breastfeeding, seeks help, and often gets misled or frightened instead. Is it any wonder so many mothers stop after a week or two? Certainly there are myriad good reasons: premature babies, poor suck, postpartum depression, low milk supply, and going back to work, to name a few. But some mothers might give up simply because it sucks, and they have been told that it's all or nothing, and they do not know that it just might, suddenly, get better.

In the end I estimate that I, who was once completely skeeved out by the very notion, nursed my three children a total of 4,325 times. I am glad that I felt the pressure to breastfeed that I did. I would never have given it a shot otherwise. And what I never could have predicted was that I would love it, and be good at it, and that it would even become easy. The blocked duct or infection that I was awaiting after Connor was born—just so I could quit—never materialized. I realize how fortunate I am to be saying that: for most women, breastfeeding is either a breeze or utter torture, but rarely anything in between. And despite swearing I'd bail at the first sign of trouble, I think I would have ridden the Feel-Bad Trolley all the way to the Supplemental Nursing System, to chronic mastitis and far beyond, rather than ever admit that I had failed. This would not have been a good thing. I admire the mother who knows when to stop doing something that really hurts, or isn't nourishing her baby sufficiently, or is making her terribly unhappy, no matter what anyone says. Every mother is different, and so is every child. How best to feed that child is something decreed by a set of circumstances that, planning and overachieving be damned, are what they are.

In my own life, breastfeeding was a gift, all three times. Despite my apprehension before I began, it became the thing about parenting I was most sure I could do well. My children remember none of our countless hours together, rocking in the glider, their little hands holding on to my breast as they drank. But I remember. For those first twelve or so months of their lives, whether my babies were hungry or sad, tired or hurt, my breasts could make everything better. If only it were all that easy.

CHAPTER SIX

Bouncing Baby Boy

One night about two weeks after Connor was born, I was nursing him on the couch, a *Law & Order* rerun burbling from the television as David and I lay there exhausted but content. The relatives, friends, and grandparents had come and gone; my breasts were no longer threatening to explode; we were, to my pleasant surprise, actually doing this. We were parents.

Then Connor stiffened his back, arched away from my breast, and let out a red-faced, four-alarm scream. "Connor! What is it?" I asked him, as if he could answer me, while David yelled, "What did you just *do*?" I remembered that one of my younger sisters had screamed like this once when I accidentally stuck her with a diaper pin while changing her. Connor wore Huggies. I checked anyway. Then I tried to nurse him again. Connor just turned his head away, still screaming. With growing panic, we swaddled him, unswaddled him, bicycled his little legs, walked him up and down. The screaming continued unabated. Just before calling 911, I offered him my breast one last time. This time, he hungrily accepted it, resuming nursing as if the previous bloodcurdling ten minutes had not occurred. David and I sank back onto the couch, looking at each other. Without each other as witnesses to what had just taken place, either of us might have thought we had merely imagined it. We hadn't.

From that evening on, my content newborn had a sudden change of disposition. The new Connor slept never and screamed always. His was no longer the typical newborn mewing, which sounds kind of cute (unless you are an engorged mother anticipating the next latch-on as one might an umpteenth waterboarding session). Connor's crying had become a piercing, unholy screech that would send him posthaste from anyone else's arms back into mine. "I think he's hungry," they'd say. "But he just ate," I'd answer, angling for just a few more moments of freedom. I never got it. Whoever was holding him could not wait to be rid of him, assuming that I, as his mother, would know how to make him stop screaming. Which I didn't.

A few days after Connor's new temperament revealed itself, David went back to work and left the two of us home alone for the first time. Connor and I were now on a ninety-minute loop, day and night, during which he would eat for thirty minutes, cry for about thirty-seven, then sleep for twenty-three. Since I was breastfeeding exclusively, no one else could take a shift, even if anyone had offered. I had therefore been managing about eighteen minutes of sleep at a time, unless something pesky like a trip to the bathroom or the intake of nourishment took up my entire allotment of sleep time for that cycle.

I figured my baby's incessant crying had to be due to something I was doing. Maybe Connor had colic, which some books suggested was a manifestation of maternal anxiety. Of course, his screaming was *why* I was so anxious, and I wasn't sure I could help that. On the other hand, maybe it was something I was *not* doing. Maybe I wasn't feeding him enough. Since I couldn't quantify my breast milk in terms of ounces served, and since nursing mothers are told to feed the baby according to his demands rather than on some draconian clock-based schedule, I could never rule hunger out. I began popping Connor back on the boob whenever he cried, even if it was three minutes after he had just finished. Sometimes he'd calm down and eat more. Maybe he had only been hungry. Maybe he was failing to thrive! Then he'd spit up all the milk from the top-off he hadn't needed after all and screech even more loudly, giving me equal conviction that I was overfeeding him. Sometimes Connor would stop right in the middle of a feeding to cry inconsolably. Well, what the hell did that mean? Did other babies cry this much? What was I doing wrong? Connor was a baby I had desperately longed for, and even when he screamed, I still adored him. But I could not ease his suffering. I was a mother who did not know how to soothe her own child.

After one particularly difficult night, I swaddled Connor and lay him in his bassinet after his 8:00 A.M. feeding. The two of us had been up the night before from 10:00 P.M. to 12:30 A.M., 2:00 to 3:30, 4:30 to 6:00, and then up at 6:30 for the day. At that point, I was hallucinating. When I put Connor down at 8:00, I was at least cogent enough to reason that if I went back to bed *right then,* Connor might give me a full ninety minutes, as tired as he was. Instead, I got ten minutes, at which point a ray of morning sunlight shone through the nursery's eastern-facing window and hit his bassinet with the focus of a magnifying-glass-wielding Webelo Scout. I called David at work, gasping, barely able to get the words out as Connor screamed in my arms. "And heee . . . he wa-as just a-sleep . . . an-d then . . . the sunliighht hit hi-i-is criiibbb . . ." David just listened. I can't do this, I said, doing a sort of daven, Connor held tight to my chest. I *can't do this*. David didn't say anything. There was nothing he could say.

The one place Connor could find an uneasy peace was in his car seat, which I could fit into his portable "Snap N Go" carriage as well as into our car. It took me a while to realize this, since it was a snowy January, the sidewalks virtually impassable for a plastic-wheeled stroller. But eventually I noticed that if Connor fell asleep in his car seat, he might nap for forty-five minutes instead of twenty-three. Since this was a nearly 100 percent improvement, Connor began taking all his naps this way, even when we were home. At night, I swaddled him tightly, plopped him in his car seat, and hoisted the whole thing into his crib, dreaming of someday stretching his nighttime rest periods to a full hour (bliss!) or more.

Sleeping in the car seat was not a practice I found supported in any of the baby books I consulted. There were warnings of restricted airways in slumping infants, and of "plagiocephaly," a flattened head that could occur in an infant who spent too much time at a forty-five-degree incline. But I had no choice. When I put Connor down on his back, he usually didn't go to sleep at all, and I would sooner have given him laudanum than put him on his stomach, since the risk of death was apparently about equal. While I fretted about the flat head thing, I fretted more about what his lack of sleep was doing to his rapidly developing brain thing. In the crib in the car seat he went. Nothing else worked. I'd tried the Baby Bjorn, three kinds of slings, the swing, the rocking chair, the bouncy chair, the vibrating chair, and putting him facedown on my lap while I patted his behind and whispered "shush, shush," in his ear, which is something some book said someone's grandmother used to do. All of these things only made Connor angrier, his tiny red fists shaking with outrage that I would even try to distract him from his afternoon's work.

The only other thing that had proven intermittently successful was a big blue exercise ball, purchased in my third trimester so that I might leisure my way through early labor in the comfort of home. During my actual labor, it sat neglected in a corner of our bedroom, and it remained there until one evening's "witching hour," the twilight moments when Connor *really* hit his stride. At the utter end of my fraying rope, I sat down on the ball with Connor and bounced him up and down. He stopped screaming. I stopped bouncing. He started screaming. I resumed bouncing and stayed there until David came home an hour and a half later.

After this accidental and wondrous discovery, we had a new evening ritual: David would get home from work, drop his papers in the doorway, and immediately begin his bouncing shift. It required a delicate handoff, since any rhythm-ceasing would send Connor into a paroxysm of rage. I would bounce one, two, three, and stand up in one motion, keeping the bouncing going as I stood there. Once David had arranged himself on the ball and assumed the rhythm, I would one, two, three, hand Connor over. We were tightrope walkers above the lion's den, defying death only by our incredible teamwork. Once the handoff had safely occurred, I would go to the kitchen drawer, grab the takeout menus, order Chinese food, answer the door when it came, shovel some down, and then take over again so David could eat. Sometimes Connor would be in a fitful sleep, far too fragile to disturb, and on those nights I would shovel forkfuls of kung pao chicken into David's mouth while he kept bouncing. This was a major breakthrough. The more vigorously we bounced Connor, the more content he seemed, as long as there was no hint of cessation. But we both knew that if for any reason we were to stop, Connor would blow up, just like that bus Sandra Bullock was driving in *Speed*.

Still, it was something, a way to stop his wailing that didn't involve one of my body parts. I was greatly relieved to have it when an audition came up the following week, a big one, to replace one of the leads in a Shakespeare play off-Broadway. (My acting career had been dormant ever since I got pregnant, so even an audition was a shot in the arm.) Since I couldn't read while bouncing without feeling carsick, I taped myself reading all the scenes and played them back while Connor and I bounced on the ball. Connor tipped his head back and listened, looking at the ceiling, as if he were trying to envision what onstage tableaux might accompany these particular lines of iambic pentameter. This audition was the very first time I would leave him. While I felt my attachment to Connor as physically as if the umbilical cord still joined us, I also felt confident in the person I was leaving him with: a kindly neighbor, a woman who had worked for years as a nurse. I instructed her in the use of the blue exercise ball, offered Connor one last milk snack, and dashed off to my audition.

I did well. I knew my lines and stayed focused, even though I could feel my breasts refilling with milk as I stood before the director, that sudden sensation of a faucet being turned on inside. I was sure my body was sensing Connor's hunger and distress from five miles away. I hurried home as soon as my audition was over, but it was the beginning of evening rush hour, and by the time I got home, I had been away for almost two hours. Connor's screams were echoing through the front door. I fumbled for my key and rushed inside. My neighbor was walking up and down with him, terrified. "Does he always cry like that?" she asked as I pulled up my shirt, Connor drinking in angry gulps.

"I'm so sorry," I said. "He must have gotten hungry."

"But he cried the entire time you were gone," she said. "And you had just fed him." The big blue ball had been useless. (She did not, evidently, have the appropriate abdominal discipline to use it; perhaps I should have pre-screened.)

"I'm so sorry," I said again. "I know he can be tough."

My neighbor looked at me, eyes wide. "It's not that," she said. "I think there might be something *wrong* with him."

There's something *wrong* with him, I told his pediatrician the next day at his four-week checkup. He cries all the time. Well, babies cry, his doctor said with an indulgent chuckle. This is different, I said. He may have colic, his doctor said, unconcerned. You'll find it happens at certain times of day, he said. (I did not.) Then he looked at Connor, who of course had chosen this five-minute consultation to be his crying break for the day, and said: Look at him, looking up at the light. What a cute little guy. Don't you worry, Mommy: things are going to get better, any day now.

They got worse. At six weeks, Connor was screaming more instead of less. During our endless days alone at home, I jazzed things up with the Dustbuster, the only thing Connor could hear above his own hundred-decibel lament. He'd stop, mid-squall, and listen with furrowed brow. I'd turn it off. He'd start crying again. I'd turn it on again. And so on. He was like the goldfish in that Ani DiFranco song: the little plastic castle was a surprise every time. Unfortunately, my short-term memory had been wiped nearly as clean.

The occasional visitor would still come by, a person I once knew, now a stranger from another world. Their visits would inevitably coincide with one of Connor's precious, hummingbird naps. They would fuss over his tiny fingernails as he dozed in the car seat, me watching them both through the glassed aquarium that had become my consciousness. I was too lobotomized to carry on a conversation. "I got a thing in the mail to get, a—you know what I mean," I told my sister Mollie, a little impatiently, as she took a turn with Connor on the big blue ball. "What you have when you belong to a museum? You buy something, and then you go whenever you want? You know that thing?"

"A *membership*?" Mollie replied cautiously, not wanting to insult me by suggesting I had a smaller vocabulary than a three-year-old.

"Yes," I said, exhaling. "Membership. I *knew* there was a word for that."

Now repeat that once a sentence. I had to use a calculator to add twelve to fourteen. I would count the minutes until David came home, so I could speak to another adult, and then be too tired to follow the thread of what he had just said to the end of his sentence. I began greeting him at the front door in wordless tears, passing Connor to him, and going to the sofa so I could sit (not bouncing) and stare at the wall.

I could not take Connor anywhere. Wherever it was, he

hated it. We left restaurants before I even ordered; we abandoned onesies on the countertop at babyGap. Any enclosed
space, whether a supermarket or an ATM, was out of the
question, and the outdoors wasn't much better. He hated our
apartment too, of course, but at least he couldn't frighten the
bejesus out of passersby (and their dogs) while we were home.
And since there wasn't anyone I could leave him with—my
kindly neighbor had stopped returning my calls—I stayed
home too. Our only field trip was to the drugstore two blocks
away, and that was the grimmest of enterprises, me grabbing
the toothpaste before the salesperson could even hand me
my receipt and rushing out of the store before Connor *really*
opened up his lungs.

One gray March morning, as I scuttled out with my toilet
paper, I spotted a flyer posted near the door:

Peggy Levine Postnatal Fitness

Underneath that, it said:

Babysitting While You Work Out!
Meet Other New Moms!

How had this neighborhood paradise escaped my notice
until now? On-premise babysitting and other mothers? Why,
there *was* a place for us! In a room full of new moms, Connor's crying would be understood—acknowledged, sure, but
with a sympathetic grin. Other moms would understand.

Connor and I were there ten minutes early for the next
morning's 9:15 A.M. offering, "New Mama Boogie." He was
asleep in his stroller when we got there, and I parked him

with the babysitter, a large African-American woman exuding capability as she presided over a dozen dozing infants. I went into the exercise room, got my step, and found a space next to a lovely English woman named Fiona. She had also just had a baby boy and lived only a few blocks away. "I don't know many other new mums," she said in her awesome accent.

"Me neither," I said. We both grinned.

Our instructor was to be the Peggy Levine of Peggy Levine Postnatal Fitness herself. I had spotted a picture of Peggy with Jane Fonda by the front door of the studio, and it seemed that Peggy had updated neither her workout outfit nor her musical selections since that time. "Let's strut our stuff, mommies!" she trumpeted, making a grand entrance in her shimmer tights to the rousing "Celebration" by Kool and the Gang. "Let's boogie off that baby weight!"

As Peggy led us through our routine, I had an unfamiliar lightness in my step. It took me a few moments to realize why: I was not bouncing on the blue ball! I was not holding anything in my arms! I swung them overhead as I hop-turned, maximizing the burn and celebrating their emptiness.

"Repeater knee, 'round the world!" Peggy yelled.

"Woo hoo!" I yelled back, along with Kool and his gang. I was free.

Just as we headed into the next song, I heard a familiar, piercing wail coming from the next room. So could everyone else; even through the wall, Connor was a good bit louder than the Pointer Sisters. Fiona and some of the other mothers faltered in their grapevines, listening with growing alarm. "Oh, don't worry!" I yelled. "He's mine. And he's fine! He's just a little tired!"

I was still grapevining to the beat when the babysitter

burst into the exercise room, in a full sweat. "Whose baby is screaming like this?" she hollered. Peggy Levine cut the Pointer Sisters. All eyes turned toward me. Face hot with cardiovascular effort and shame, I walked toward the babysitter and took Connor back. As I could have predicted, this did not really help. "Put him to the breast, child," the babysitter said gently, as if to an imbecile. I sat against the mirrored wall, pulled up my sports bra, and attempted to latch him on. Connor twisted away from me, screaming, my let-down milk spraying him in the face and enraging him even further. "He's *not hungry*," I hissed at the babysitter, Peggy Levine, and the room in general, and went to get his stroller. Everyone watched, horrified, as I stuffed the demon child back in his snowsuit, wheeling him outside so he could worship his Dark Master in peace. *Good-bye, Fiona,* I thought. *I will never forget you.*

Back at home (a prisoner again) I began noting Connor's sleeping and eating "patterns" on a chart, having just read that a baby without a schedule was a baby whose mother was not paying enough attention. I was to record everything Connor did, sleeping hours shaded in pencil, waking hours left white, feedings noted by a star. This would, this expert promised, show how even a ten-week-old baby was creating his or her own schedule: waking once a night to be fed, nursing maybe six times during the day, taking four or so daily naps. On the weekend Connor was ten weeks old, according to my records, he nursed six times a *night* and took eight daily naps of ten minutes apiece.

Granted, this was a particularly bad weekend, since we had taken our possessed child out of his element and brought him to our hometown of Scranton, Pennsylvania, to attempt an exorcism. Connor was to be baptized in the same church where I received First Communion and where David and I had been married. Afterward, we were hosting a brunch for fifty friends and relatives. That morning, on thirteen minutes' sleep, I bounced Connor on the big blue ball in his white christening gown. (We had, of course, deflated and packed the ball for our trip to Scranton; I would sooner have left Connor behind than that ball.) Since the ball might have been deemed an inappropriate accessory for the moment Connor was washed in the waters of salvation, I was giving him some extra-vigorous bouncing before we left for church. On this particular day, though, not even the ball could stay Connor from swift completion of his appointed howls. Connor's paternal grandmother (christened "YaYa" by the oldest grandchild) stood in the doorway and watched me bounce, a little too forcefully. "He screamed *all night*," YaYa said, incredulous.

"That's what he does," I answered, not even looking up at her. By now, I well knew I had the worst baby in the world; I was just tired of having that pointed out to me.

YaYa proceeded tentatively, as any good mother-in-law should. "Maybe," she said, "you should get him checked out."

After the baptism and the brunch, which my body attended but my brain did not, my mother (reveling in her new role as "Nana") offered to mind Connor at her house while I napped in the guest room. After two hours of dreamless, drooling coma, I went back downstairs to find Connor staring at the kitchen lights, Nana holding him away from her with her fingertips, like a grenade. Under normal circumstances, my mother would rather cut out her tongue than express an unpleasant truth. "I don't know," Nana began, gingerly. "I think he might need to go to the doctor's."

I went back to the pediatrician that Monday. This time I asked to see a different member of the practice. "There's something *wrong* with him," I said. The doctor regarded me hesitantly. I was just another unhinged new mother, a Cassandra, doomed to possess the truth without being able to convince anyone who could help. "His grandmothers *said*," I continued. "*Both* of them. Please."

The doctor vacillated. "Colic can be very hard," she said.

"This isn't colic!" I answered, cutting her off. "You have to believe me! Look!" I pulled out Connor's sleeping charts, pages and pages of them, random like computer punch cards, the confetti non-pattern of our days. She looked at them, then up at me. She gave me a referral.

Dr. Desciak was among the best pediatric gastroenterologists in the field, and saw no need to waste his time with pleasantries. He took Connor from me, laid him on his back, and vigorously palpated his tiny torso, Connor too confused to protest. He assessed Connor's poopy diaper for some time. Then, finally, he spoke:

DR. DESCIAK: Does he sleep at night?
ME: No, Doctor. He's worse at night. I have some charts—
DR. DESCIAK: Does he stop in the midst of nursing to cry?
ME: All the time.
DR. DESCIAK: Does he tip his head back and look up at the ceiling?

Well, that was spooky.

ME: Yes. He does. He likes to look at the lights.

That was all Dr. Desciak needed to hear. There was a flap at the top of Connor's esophagus, he explained, that the vagaries of prenatal development had left less than fully formed. Therefore, the contents of Connor's stomach were washing back up into his throat, creating a fire of pain at regular intervals. Connor was tipping his head back in an attempt to keep the acid down. Lying on his back, allowing the acid to flow freely, was baby torture.

Double waves of relief (from finding out what was wrong) and guilt (from wondering what had taken me so long) crashed over me as Dr. Desciak issued his physician's orders:

- Two milliliters of Zantac, twice a day.
- Keep Connor upright as much as possible, even when he was asleep.

Most important, as long as I breastfed, I was to
- Remove every trace of dairy from my diet.

Dr. Desciak told me this last part as if he expected some resistance. But I would have gladly restricted my diet to occasional nibbles of cardboard if I thought it would make Connor sleep for four hours at a stretch. I dove into label-reading that very evening, tossing the offending soups and salad dressings in our pantry that had by-products of whey lurking deep within their lists of ingredients. I shopped at the kosher market for products marked "pareve," a word that had in the past caught only my passing fancy on a bag of pretzels but that was now of direst importance, designating a food as dairy-free, as safe. I held Connor completely vertical against my shoulder as he napped four times a day. I administered the Zantac, which I knew tasted terrible from its leavings on my fingers as I filled the syringe, but which Connor took without complaint. Maybe he too hoped that one of these things, or all of them, might begin to work, slowly but surely.

After a month of breast milk without a trace of cow milk in it, Connor napped for two hours. In his crib. Without the car seat. After two months, Dr. Desciak cut the Zantac to once daily. After three months, Connor began eating rice cereal, devouring tablespoons of it at each feeding, smiling broadly at me as I loaded his spoon with the next bite. After eleven months, I treated myself to pizza for dinner and tore off some tiny bites for Connor to chase around his high-chair tray with his fat little hands. Both of us slept until morning.

Change does happen. I read somewhere that the human body totally regenerates every seven years, that over that time, every cell in the body replaces itself, and there is no part of you left that was there seven years ago. Over seven years, you become someone completely different.

Connor will be seven this December. He begs me for ice cream every time we pass the Mr. Softee truck parked, as soon as the temperature hits 60, right where we get off the downtown bus together after school. His stomach seems to tolerate the Spider-Man frozen dairy product bar (with black gumball eyes) quite nicely. Before bedtime, I sit with him on his twin bed, trading pages as we read *Danny and the Dinosaur*. He squints at his page, sounding out the word "taught." As Connor concentrates, I reach up out of habit and rub the flat spot on the back of his head. The books' warning came true: Baby Connor got moderate plagiocephaly from all those months sleeping in his car seat. But now, almost seven years later, the spot has shrunk enough so you cannot really see it. I am the only one who knows where to find it under my son's thick hair. As Connor reads to me, I rub his flat spot for luck, and remember that the tempestuous first months of his life— as fuzzy to me now as real life was then—really did, after all, happen.

CHAPTER SEVEN

My Book of Faces

I have a good friend named Julie, whose every word I cling to for any scrap of coolness I might salvage from it. Julie is child-free and is my primary tether to the halcyon days of regular workout schedules and first-run movies, of sleeping in Saturday morning and going out Saturday night without having to factor in another $65 for the babysitter. (Julie likes to remind me that since she works two jobs, her life is not exactly the one of ease and leisure that I imagine. I say, don't mess with my fantasy.)

When I manage to escape the house and spend time with Julie, she lets drop effortlessly urbanista tips on the perfect comfortable-but-cool boots, the latest concealer, and what I should have on my iPod. "I like Florence and the Machine," she'll mention, and I nod, pretending to have ever heard of them, and make a mental note to download some of their music one of these days, just as soon as I file all the health claim forms from 2003 I've been meaning to get to.

Last summer, I was attempting to speak to Julie on the

phone. I had my two youngest, overheated children clamped to each of my legs, clamoring for my attention with that panicked immediacy children only acquire when they see their mother with a telephone to her ear. "This is why I have no friends," I said. "I can't talk to someone for thirty seconds."

"You should be on Facebook!" Julie said.

I thought she was trying to be funny.

"Seriously, Ame," she said. "It's not college kids anymore. You'd love it."

This would probably be one of those cases where Julie's coolness far exceeded mine, like the time I attempted to rock these old lady sandals from Germany that had looked much cuter on her. I assumed Facebook would be a bunch of youngsters "chatting" with winking emoticons, sending urgent missives like "CU L8R!!!" Since I abhor excessive use of the exclamation point above all other things, I was almost certainly too old for this newfangled communication medium. But that evening, once the kids were in bed and the laundry was folded, I decided to enter my e-mail address so Facebook could whirr and click its way through my Yahoo! contact list. Then, bam! Up came fifty people or more whom I knew, all already using Facebook, most of whom I had lost touch with long ago. Here was that cute novelist I went to college with! Here was that kind of famous actor I kind of knew! I "friended" them all, and they "friended" me back, and by the next evening I was trading witty banter with all the cool people I used to know, as if at a giant cocktail party, only without the trouble of putting on makeup beforehand.

I gorged on Facebook every night after the kids were asleep, furiously refreshing for real-time updates. Here was a girl I went to grade school with, saying she just saw one of the

"Real Housewives of New York" at TJ Maxx! Here was that guy who sublet my apartment thirteen years ago, asking me to take the "Which Character on *Full House* Are You?" quiz. Some of these topics were, admittedly, less than scintillating. But I was wallowing in my new sense of community. A week earlier, the only people I had contact with were the moms I waved to at camp drop-off. Now I was back in touch with friends from all chapters of my life! Sort of! Still, wasn't it better to choose a virtual plant for my college roommate's Li'l Green Patch than not to be in touch with her at all? I would never have time to catch up fully with all these people, but now I wouldn't have to. I would hear the highlights of their lives going forward, and I'd never have to feel isolated again. I was enchanted with my many, many Friends.

The only part of Facebook that had me fraught with anxiety was the choosing of my profile photo. I had been going with no photo at all for a few weeks, which seemed like a safe choice. But in actuality, the shadowy blue no-face lady next to your name merely brands you as a Facebook neophyte. Even I, a Facebook neophyte, could see that. But there were so many ways to get the photo wrong that indecision stayed my hand. If I used an overly glamorous or professionally taken photo of myself, my narcissism would be on display for everyone I had ever met. So I attempted a self-portrait, holding my cell phone above my head at an insouciant angle like my college sophomore cousin had, and got a horrifying "before" picture such as one might see in a magazine makeover story. If I used *that* picture, the apparent toll the last seven years had taken on me would be evident to everyone I had ever met. I needed to find an accidentally terrific candid shot, one in which I looked great without looking like I was *trying* to look great. I spent the next several nights after the kids were asleep sifting through every digital photo stored on my computer, and found a handful of options:

- a photo of me in the hospital delivery room, taken immediately after Seamus was born, with IV-bloated face and burst blood vessels in my eyes
- a photo from the previous Christmas morning, my matted hair and dark-circled eyes a testament to how long it takes to put the Fisher-Price Planet Heroes Solar Headquarters together (without instructions)
- a photo of me on my birthday the year before, seven months pregnant, "glowing" with forehead acne, and my eyes half-closed

That was about it. If you were to piece together our family's story based on our photos, you would think that our three children had raised themselves and some scary sweaty fat lady stopped by once or twice a year.

I broadened my search criteria from a good photo of me, to any photo of me, to any photo in which some part of my head appeared, and finally found something acceptable: a picture of our whole family at the pool, the boys hamming it up, me in the background behind hat and sunglasses. Shrunk down to Facebook's thumbnail size, you could barely see me in the photo. Eh, it was fine; my kids were my biggest news since the millennium, anyhow. I did wonder, though, if it was wise to broadcast "I am a boring mother with nothing to say" to all of my Friends without children. Sometimes I get the sense that not only do people without children not want to hear about my kids, they might actually think *less* of me for having them.

Before kids, I had a pretty successful career as an actress, and I had stories about meeting Woody Allen and Warren Beatty fit for any occasion. Now, when someone asks me, "What do you do?" I don't necessarily want to say, "I'm an actress," since that will beg the question of what they've seen me in, which is, recently, nothing. Instead, I go with the job that has kept me most consistently busy for the last seven years. "I'm a mom," I say, and then I see the switch go off behind their eyes: *Oh. Uninteresting, not smart, and now that I look at her, I guess she is kind of frumpy.*

I remember feeling that way myself a decade ago when David would take me to work-sponsored events. He works in the financial industry, a male-dominated world where they are politically correct enough to call their companions "spouses," even though we are all, in fact, wives. I would work the room with David at one of these cocktail parties, or sit at these dinners, and dread when his conversation, as it inevitably did, would turn to matters financial. He and his coworkers would begin speaking in jargon that was completely incomprehensible to me (and still is).

DAVID: Did we traunch that mezz piece out yet?
OTHER GUY: Yep. Twenty over forty, margin EBITDA.
DAVID: Who's on the left?
OTHER GUY: Us, less fifteen basis points top three.
DAVID: Well, let's diligence that out.

Once this sort of talk started it would always continue uninterrupted through the end of the evening, icing me out completely. David had tried to explain what he was talking about to me many times, but just because you take high school French doesn't mean you'll understand a word they say in Paris, either.

That meant I would have to turn to the "spouses" at the table, the other women who were as squeezed out of the work conversation as I was. It never seemed to bother them much, though. They'd have plenty to talk about: their second grader's traveling soccer team, their Parents' Association obligations, and the Italian tile for their kitchen backsplash that had been lost in customs and was setting their renovation back by six weeks or more. I would sit there nodding and smiling, and while at least they were speaking English, it wasn't like this sort of talk was really any better. I had nothing to say about runny noses and Uba Tuba granite countertops, and I was proud of it! Seriously, who were these women? Didn't they ever watch the news or read a book? Didn't they understand how very uninteresting all of this was? Did they really think anyone else cared?

Now, ten years later, I have drunk the Stepford Kool-Aid, and I do great at these parties. Sure, I read the newspaper, but the subjects on top of my brain-pile are the minutiae of my daily life as a mother, and when I am in a room with other mothers, these topics are universal, noncontroversial, and endlessly regenerating. It's only when I catch a glimpse of myself through the eyes of someone without children that I share in the horror of just what has become of me.

David's younger sister Kelly and her boyfriend Chris came over to visit a few years ago. It was a charity visit; David was out of town on a business trip and both boys had a stomach bug. Aunt Kelly tucked the boys in and read them bedtime stories while I gave the bathroom a good sanitizing. I followed Kelly and Chris to the front door once the boys were asleep, not ready yet to let these beguiling visitors from the Land of the Childless leave me. I started in on what I thought was a hilarious monologue about the color and extent of baby Seamus's diarrhea that afternoon. "I mean, it was like Jell-O pudding! And yellow!" I brayed. I saw Kelly and Chris cast a furtive look at each other. Not even an eye roll. More like: *On my signal, run for your life, before she eats our brains.*

This was why my Facebook photo choice was a little bit risky. If a mother wants to sojourn in the non-child-centered world, she is better off keeping her Shutterfly brag books tucked securely away. The ideal of the woman who "has it all" is predicated on that woman keeping her worlds totally separate. She doesn't begin meetings talking about how the baby can sing "Old MacDonald." She doesn't close the deal with a raucous breast pump anecdote. We mothers can continue to participate in grown-up society only if we don't let our mothering lives leak into our professional lives. We are of interest to the real world only to the extent that we don't remind anyone of *our* real world. We mothers, like our children, are supposed to know our place.

I'm not sure why there is such little patience shown for mothers. If I bring my little yappy dog into a coffee shop, I can see people being miffed. But a crying baby? I'll back his stroller out of there and be on my way as quickly as I can, but honestly, he's a human being too. Adults who have no tyke tolerance did not, as they seem to believe, spring fully formed from the forehead of Zeus. All cranky adults were once cranky kids, and when they cried (as clearly they did; their dispositions speak for themselves), they were annoying too.

And so are mothers, I hear the non-child-centered saying in response. I do have some sympathy for how they might have lost their patience. First we clogged the sidewalks with our double strollers, now we clog the news feeds. And even I think that mom who uploads thirty-seven photos of her son's Little League banquet, one at a time, onto the Facebook pages of everyone she knows, needs to be stopped. She's making us all look bad.

But why shouldn't we mothers talk about our lives, even when among the childless? Hell, there's a lot to discuss, and most of it is a lot more interesting than the articles we wrote for law review. Just because a topic is grown-up doesn't make it interesting; I once talked to an astrophysicist who bored me to death. But I didn't groan inwardly as soon as he *told* me he was an astrophysicist, thinking, *Oh God, this guy's sure to be a snore*. The entire topic of motherhood is considered not worth one's time unless one is a mother, and maybe not even then. Motherhood is still seen as a waste of a smart woman's mind, as if motherhood were beneath her talents, rather than the job that most requires every ounce of strength and ingenuity that she possesses. How each mother negotiates that is, in my opinion, a topic of endless variety.

Still, once we mothers get the sense that the friends from our old lives don't really want to hear it, we gravitate toward those who do. As a result, every friend I have made in the last seven years became my friend because she was a fellow mother. Whenever I talk to these women, whether at karate pickup, work dinners, or girls' night margaritas, we have tons to discuss: spelling tests, swine flu, and why our husbands leave their dirty dishes in the sink rather than in the immediately adjacent dishwasher. What we almost never talk about, though, are the lives that we left behind when our kids arrived, or are struggling to maintain now that they're here. We stick with the parts of each other with which we are already familiar. Right now, we don't have enough energy left for anything else. While these friends understand what has become the largest part of me, they do not know who I was before motherhood, or who I hope to be once my kids don't need me anymore. I am still left with things I am yearning to say.

And so I find myself coming home after a night out with the old playgroup gang and logging on to Facebook one more time before bed, where I can be mother, writer, sister, theater geek, 80s trivia champion, and confidante, or all of them at once, to some of my three hundred Friends. I wait to speak up until I have something witty, provocative, or at least charming to say. Then I shout into the void: "Amy thinks the movie *Diner* is overrated." "Amy wants a chocolate milkshake." And sometimes no one answers. But sometimes, the person who responds is someone whom I never could have predicted.

David says he'll never join Facebook. I think he's probably right. But his life hasn't changed like mine has in the last seven years. He has gotten to stay the same him all this time. David also says I spend too much time on Facebook and I should get a good night's sleep instead. He is certainly spot-on there. Why am I staying up till all hours to read whether the woman who stage-managed my high school plays prefers Goobers or Raisinets?

But the funny thing is, it's kind of nice to know. She likes Raisinets better. A moment later, there I am, peeking out from behind my children in my photo, saying: so do I. For just a moment we are heard by each other, her life intersecting, once again, with mine.

CHAPTER EIGHT

Translocation

Staying home with a toddler will lead to some of the longest, most meandering afternoons of your life. After nap time, you've got five hours to fill (best-case scenario) until it's time for night-night, and when it's been raining for three days straight, you yearn for a little excitement. Something. Anything. Such are the moments, once interrupted, that you rue having wished away.

The phone only rarely rang in the afternoon, and I remember thinking, first, that it was strange to be getting a call at all. "Hello?" I panted, since I had been giving Connor horsey rides around the house, and in my second trimester of my second pregnancy, shortness of breath was already in full swing. Seventeen weeks, and I looked and felt more like thirty.

"Hi, Amy, it's Mary? From Dr. Merman's office?"

"Oh, hi, Mary—Connor, couches are not for jumping!" Dr. Merman was my obstetrician, and Mary was probably calling to reschedule an appointment or something. "Sorry. How are you, Mary?"

"I'm fine," she said, and I thought it was a little strange that she didn't ask me how I was, or "the babies," as she usually did. Mary had been with me from the very beginning of my journey to motherhood, and she was a lot like my own mother, except for the flat Queens accent. They shared a sunny and unflappable Irish Catholic disposition. When it came to my body, and the making of babies, Mary actually knew a lot more than my mother did. While still on my odyssey of infertility, I would go to Dr. Merman's office month after month, cry in the waiting room, and have yet more blood taken. Only Mary could find a good vein and get it over with without me seeing black spots. She worked quickly, chattering away the entire time, and allowed me to feel that everything might yet be okay.

When my second pregnancy caught me completely by surprise, I called Mary from my bathroom, the pregnancy test still unsanitarily wet in my hand, Connor crawling around on the floor. "I think I'm *pregnant*," I whispered, too shocked to say it out loud. "You get over here right now!" Mary said, laughing, even though it was already four thirty in the afternoon. Upon treating my urine sample, she confirmed my suspicions with a wink and a congratulatory punch on the arm. She let Connor play with the paper clips on her desk while Dr. Merman examined me and declared me healthily super-pregnant. I hadn't even told David yet, but Mary knew. Between Mary and me, there was very little to hide.

Now I stood in my den, hoisting Connor on one hip so he would stop face-diving off the sofa. "I'm calling with the results of your amnio," Mary said.

"Oh, right," I said. I had forgotten.

This was my first amniocentesis, ordered only because

the results of my prenatal blood work had shown a one in two hundred chance that the fetus might have Down syndrome. These were higher odds than might be expected for a woman of my age, although still pretty remote. I was not that concerned. Growing up in Scranton, Pennsylvania, where everyone is Catholic, I had known a handful of families with Down syndrome kids. I wasn't blind to the challenges of such a life, but it wasn't a complete unknown to me, either. For me, it was something I could face, as long as I had time to prepare. "Let's just check the box," Dr. Merman had said. "Let's know for sure."

A week later, I got the amnio. David said it was a good thing I had kept my eyes closed because the needle Dr. Merman inserted into my womb was, quote, "freaking *long*." I held my breath and meditated on my healthy womb, my healthy baby, the needle staying far away. In a moment, it was over, having hurt less than a bug bite, and I felt such extreme relief that the procedure had gone well that I had forgotten about the reasons I had had the test in the first place.

Mary said, again, "So I have your results," and I figured she was just in a hurry because she had someone else holding on the other line.

"So, good," I said. "Are we good?"

She didn't say anything for a moment.

"You and David need to come into our office this afternoon," she said finally.

I clutched the arm of the couch. "Okay," I said, as calmly as I could. And hung up. I didn't press Mary for more information. Clearly, I didn't want to.

I vaguely remember calling my friend Debbie and hijacking our shared babysitter for the afternoon. Then I called

David at work, another rare phone call in the middle of the day. He was always insanely busy, so what was the point? David and I had a long-standing agreement: while he didn't have time to chat, he would always pick up my call, under any circumstance, if I told his assistant I really needed him. As long as I didn't have her do it unless it was something really important. Until now, I never had. "I need to speak to David right now," I told her, trying to keep the shake out of my voice.

I plopped Connor in front of a rerun of *Lassie* (his favorite show) and got in the shower, because even though it was two in the afternoon, I hadn't done anything to make myself presentable to the outside world. Until the phone rang, I hadn't had anywhere I needed to go. I had to reach up and steady myself against the slippery, wet wall. *Just take the shower,* I told myself. *You know how to do this. You can get through these next two minutes.* I rubbed the soap in circles, moving down my body and reaching my abdomen, which had already relaxed well into the Definitely Pregnant stage. Anyone could see there was a baby in there—it was not a secret, not an abstraction. My baby was real, and there was something terribly wrong.

From above, I watched myself put on the maternity pants, hand Connor off to the babysitter, and take a cab across town to Dr. Merman's office. David met me in the waiting room, his face gray, his hand cold when he took mine. Mary was uncharacteristically silent, busying herself with the papers on her desk. After a few moments Dr. Merman opened his office door and called us in.

I had found Dr. Merman through a friend who was also a patient. She used to call him "Doctor Mister Rogers" because of the soothing monotone in which he spoke. I had always felt safe with Dr. Merman's reassuring manner, grandfatherly age, and apparent vast experience. Whatever bumps we hit—unexplained infertility, endometriosis, an umbilical cord around the neck during delivery—we could put our trust in Dr. Merman, who had dealt with all of these things a hundred times before.

"The results of your amnio show what is called a 'genetic translocation,'" Dr. Merman explained, once we were seated across from him. "Sometimes, as the chromosomes are forming, they break apart. When they rejoin themselves, it may not be in the same place."

I had forgotten how to breathe. I imagined helixes dangling, stuck to each other like flypaper, tangled beyond repair.

"Now, your baby has what is called a *balanced* translocation," Dr. Merman continued, gently. "All the necessary genetic material is present. It's just not in its usual location."

"So . . . what is the problem?" David said. (He would do the talking.)

"There may not even be a problem," Dr. Merman answered. "But we have to test both of you to find out. If one of you has the same translocation in your DNA, then it's inherited, and since you've made it to healthy adulthood, we can assume that the mutation is inconsequential. But if this is occurring in your baby for the first time, then it becomes a little more complicated. It could be a sign of severe disabilities."

"How many times have you seen something like this?" David asked. (He wanted the stats; numbers were what he could wrap his head around.)

"Twice before," Dr. Merman said. "Once it turned out fine."

We were all silent for a moment.

"We are going to get both of you tested today," Dr. Merman said, closing the folder. "There is about a sixty percent chance that one of you has this same aberration; in that case, we can assume that it will be nothing. Even if neither of you has it, there's still a sixty percent chance that the mutation will cause only developmental disabilities. The baby might be slow learning to walk, or have trouble learning to read."

"How would we know what kind of disability it would be?" David asked.

"We wouldn't," Dr. Merman said. "You would have no way of knowing until the baby was born."

"So on the forty percent chance of the forty percent chance there's something really wrong with the baby," David said, pressing him, "what would we be looking at then?"

"In that case, you would want to consider the possibility of terminating," Dr. Merman admitted, using a euphemism that did not really soften the blow.

I cried quietly while Mary took my blood. I forgot to notice whether it hurt or not. "I'm so sorry," she whispered.

"It will take ten days to get your test results," Dr. Merman told us by way of farewell. "In the meantime, I recommend you seek genetic counseling."

Instead, David and I went home, sat in front of the television without watching it, and told no one. What was there to say? That there might be some undefined but horrible thing wrong with the baby we had announced months ago? And that we could not know how really horrible things were for another week and a half?

No option seemed thinkable. How could I consider ending a pregnancy with only a 40 percent chance of severe defects? What if I guessed wrong, and the baby might have been fine?

On the other hand, what if the baby were born with defects beyond medicine's capacities? Down syndrome would have at least been something that we could research, that we could wrap our heads around. Granted, these questions were the reason genetic counseling existed. But what could be less comforting than discussing a variety of worst-case scenarios we could neither confirm nor deny?

"No two translocations are the same," Dr. Merman had said. "They are infinitely complicated." Like snowflakes. And since our snowflake still had a 60 percent chance of being healthy, we chose not to talk about it for those ten days, at least as much as possible. "I'd take three out of five odds in Vegas any day," David said, which was a good point, even if he didn't say it with much conviction. We'd joke about which one of us might turn out to have the screwed-up DNA and how it would have manifested itself. I said it was surely him, since he had distant relatives with an entire extra set of teeth impacted in their jaws. Surely it was me, he argued, since my whole family had the "Ferguson tail," where our hair grew to a neat point at the nape of the neck. Weren't these quirks written on our DNA somehow? Might not all yet be well?

On another quiet afternoon with Connor ten days later, only this one jangling with tension, the phone rang again. "It's you," Mary said, as soon as I answered. "Thank God. You have it too. Everything is going to be fine." We called our parents that night when David came home from work, our deliverance bubbling over. You have no idea, we said, how hard this has been. But there's no reason to worry! The baby has it, but Amy also has it, and Connor might even have it also, and we're all fine. My mother-in-law tried to catch up on our ten-day lead of anxiety and release. "Wait. If Connor has it, wouldn't they have caught it when you were pregnant with him?" she asked.

"Well, no," I answered, " because I didn't *have* an amnio with him." Huh.

It hadn't occurred to me until that moment: there had never really been any reason to worry. If I hadn't had the amniocentesis, it all might have been avoided, since I would never have known to panic over a nonissue in the first place. After all, it seemed that I had had this defect myself while in my own mother's womb, but she never agonized over it, because she never had the tests. The amnio had created the crisis, giving me half-baked disaster scenarios that had put me on the ledge, and needlessly so.

I called my five brothers and sisters to let them know they probably had this abnormality also. This way, if it came up in their own prenatal testing, they would know not to worry. But on the other end of the phone, I could hear less relief than puzzlement. How was one supposed to react to this news? There is a mutation inside you—but it's meaningless. Have a great weekend!

Having been declared mutation-free, David was punchy with relief, teasing Mary at our next ultrasound. "I bet you hated making *that* phone call," he said.

"Oh, Lord Almighty," Mary replied. "Let me tell you, it was awful. But it's better to know."

Really, though, it wasn't.

Before this all happened, Mary had asked me if we would take the genetics-clad certainty the amnio provided to find out what we were having. I said no, but later events had changed my mind. If everything turned out all right, our reward would be to know this baby fully. If we had to learn everything about it, the chambers of its heart counted, the strands of its DNA unraveled and examined, then it seemed only logical to get this one last piece of trivia: what kind of baby it would be.

After all the testing was done and the baby declared healthy—as it had been all along—Mary gave me an envelope to open with David at home. This one last time, she knew more about my baby than anyone else. Even me. "It's a boy!" Mary wrote in her parochial-school cursive. "Congratulations!" I remember trying to show some excitement, hoisting flutes of sparkling cider with David to celebrate, but feeling only a numbness that the crisis was past. Whether the baby was a boy or a girl seemed so inconsequential compared to the relief that he would be whole.

A pregnant woman seeks comfort in her visits to the obstetrician, the reassurance that everything is all right. But these days, she is much more likely to find something to worry about there: only one side of the baby's umbilical cord is transporting blood, and it might be fine, or it might not. Your baby has a cyst, and it might be benign, and it might not. What cannot be known still far outstrips what can.

I had been lucky. The pieces of my baby had come apart, dangled, and then come back together. Everything was still there, if a bit shuffled. Sometimes, though, I still peer at Seamus as he plays, as he sleeps, looking for the quirk that he and I share. I have not yet found it, but it must be there somewhere. We are translocated, he and I, and I still wonder if it is, one of these days, going to reveal why it is there.

CHAPTER NINE

Meaningful Montessori

There is a particular brand of frantic that attends the first time since giving birth that a mother of a newborn has to get out of the house and be somewhere before 9:00 A.M. It doesn't matter if it's your first baby or not. When you have a second child, you know how to cope with the exhaustion. Heck, you can even manage to handle two under two most of the time. What you can't handle is putting on makeup and blow-drying your hair for the first time since your water broke, plus trying on everything in your closet looking in vain for something that fits and that you don't look still-pregnant in.

About six weeks after my second child was born, I was in the kitchen, nursing Seamus for the seventh time since 4:00 A.M. while making a sippy cup of watered-down juice for Connor, then one and a half, whose overnight diaper sagged to his knees. David shuffled into the kitchen in his boxers, rubbing his eyes. "Why are you not dressed?!" I shrieked. "I have three people to worry about! You have *one*! We cannot be late! Will you just *put your clothes on*!" After finding something in my postpartum, indeterminate size that would look serious but not desperate, corporate but not snobby, we met the babysitter at the door, handed over two crying babies, and rushed out to hail a cab. What could be so terribly urgent, you ask? Only a meeting where Connor's *entire future* would be decided. Where he would go to college, his level of success— why, his very ability to pursue happiness—were about to be determined. All by his parents' ten-minute interview at the Meaningful Montessori of Manhattan.

Although Connor had only been walking for a few months, our family was hip-deep in the application process to nursery school in New York City. Actually, schools. Okay, nine. Nine! Sound unreasonable? Only until you understand that it is statistically easier for your child to get into Harvard than into the Shining Time Nursery on the Upper West Side. (And only a little bit more expensive.) The number of kids under five in Manhattan has increased by almost half in the last ten years, and so nursery schools have to choose among hundreds of applicants for the handful of spots that aren't already promised to siblings of current students or "legacy" children of alumni. (That's "sibs" and "legs," to parents in the know.) If Jesus Christ were alive today, he'd skip the business about the camel and the eye of a needle and just say that it is easier to get into Little Big Apples on Lexington Avenue than for a rich man to get into heaven. And all the people on the Mount of Olives would be like, "Ohhh. That's *really* bad."

In Scranton, Pennsylvania, when I had just turned four, my grandmother heard about a nursery school at a church where our neighbor worked, and she walked me in the first day. That's where I went. My parents didn't apply anywhere else. Heck, I'm not sure they "applied" there. I might have just shown up. Why would they have looked elsewhere? It was a room with little chairs, other kids, nice ladies, and finger paint. Those were the only criteria most of our parents were working from—that is, if they sent us to preschool at all.

And I'm not saying that was bad. That was good. That was sane. It was ridiculous to think Connor's path in life would be determined before he could speak in complete sentences. I hadn't gone to a designer preschool, and I had found gainful employment, had I not? So I was not going to lose my mind over where Connor played with blocks three mornings a week. I didn't care where he went. The only problem was, I wanted him to go *somewhere,* and that was by no means a foregone conclusion.

This was why David and I were about to attend nine school tours, nine parental interviews, and nine open houses/curriculum nights/"head of school forums," whatever those were. This meant eighteen mornings as panicked as this one had been, and for David, it meant skipping eighteen mornings at work. I would tolerate no opposition from him on this. According to the moms on the urbanbaby.com message boards, there was no way I could go alone. "If both parents aren't at the interview, they will interpret that as a lack of commitment to the school," one mother explained. "These schools are just looking for a reason to throw your application away. Don't make it *that* easy."

So there David and I were at our first interview, a little sweaty from our morning's exertion but on time. Meaningful Montessori's head of admissions glanced at us over her half glasses and indicated we could sit in the two uncomfortable-looking plastic chairs opposite her desk. We sat knock-kneed, watching her as she glanced over Connor's application. I saw another toddler's application atop the pile on her desk; it was typed. Shit. I had printed!

Describe your child's use of language.

That was a tough question to lead off with, since as I have already made clear, Connor was then what the specialists would call "preverbal."

"Connor can say 'Hi'!" I wrote in my neatest Palmer method. "And 'Mommy' and 'Daddy'!"

Unfortunately, there were still three blank lines, beckoning for more.

"Connor also knows what the horsey says," I wrote. "In fact, he is fluent in all barnyard animal sounds."

Still more space.

"He uses language . . . in a manner quite appropriate for his age," I finished with a flourish, hoping that sounded like a parent who made sure of such things.

How much TV does your child watch?

"One hour in the morning, and half an hour before bed," I wrote confidently, proud of myself for never succumbing to a midday Diego marathon. Then I remembered that since Connor was not yet two, the only correct answer, according to the American Academy of Pediatrics, was "None." Since a cross-out would have been too glaringly obvious, I appended, "On weekends, that is."

How does your child express anger?

Was this a trick question? Was I supposed to say, "He doesn't"? Because Connor threw tantrums that could be heard in Europe. Concluding that the broadly descriptive phrase "terrible twos" must mean there were more like him, I admitted that Connor did get mad at times, but in a really, really advanced and school-ready way. "Connor tells me he has an 'angry message' for me," I wrote smoothly, "and then we role-play with hand puppets."

When does your child go to bed?

Now, see, why did that matter? That was my decision as a parent, not Connor's. Then a shiver went down my spine as I saw it all clearly: *none* of these questions were about my son. They were all about me. What kind of mother I was. The parenting decisions I had made had shaped my child, and it was those decisions that were under the microscope. Each of them. *All* of them. In order for these educational professionals to decide if Connor would be good enough for their school, everything I had ever done as a mother was fair game.

At what age did your child sleep through the night?

"Ten months," I admitted, then recovered with "because he had reflux." I figured the sleepless nights that came with the gastroesophageal issues were finally paying off here, giving me some extra points. Then, when I considered that "reflux" could be interpreted as "child rendered high-maintenance by his hypochondriac-by-proxy mother," I quickly added, "he's better now."

At what age was your child weaned?

"Eleven months." By now, I was second-guessing all my answers. Was that too short? Too long? Had I truncated his future brain development by not making it to a year? Had I created an overly dependent child by being the last mom in our playgroup to wean?

Was it a vaginal birth?

Oh. Yes. They. Did. Ask. That.

I wanted to write "None of your beeswax," but if Connor was going to get in, I had to answer all of these questions, no matter how humiliating. At least I could answer yes. I hadn't read any studies suggesting that C-section babies were less likely to share in the dress-up corner, but this question made me certain such studies were out there. (Unless the studies actually indicated that the trauma of a baby's trip through the birth canal was detrimental to right-brain reasoning.) For most of the questions, it was hard to know what to say, because I wasn't sure what it was they wanted to hear. What was the *right* time to put your child to bed? 7:15 P.M.? 7:30 P.M.? 6:48 P.M.?

The doyenne of Meaningful Montessori gave a cursory finger-trace over our application, her face revealing nothing.

"So. You are applying your son . . . Connor."

"Yes," I said, flashing an energetic grin, hoping that my name choice for my firstborn was acceptable.

"How old will he be?"

"Two!" I answered. In person, at least, the questions were easy.

"Two point oh?"

I didn't get it. Was she making some kind of software joke? No, she wasn't smiling. It was an actual question.

"No . . . two and a half," I answered.

"Two point *six*?" she pressed. Was she testing my decimal skills? How much was six tenths of a twelve-month year? My mind was reeling.

"Is that two and a half?" I said, chuckling, trying to at least appear jovial in addition to stupid.

Ms. Montessori sighed wearily. "How many years and how many months will your child be next September?" she asked.

"Two years . . . and nine months," I stammered.

"Two point nine," Ms. Montessori concluded. She frowned slightly and made a faint mark on Connor's application.

"Is that all right?" David asked.

"I'll be frank. It's not ideal. We prefer young threes."

"He will be *almost* three," I pointed out in what I hoped was a helpful tone.

"Two point elevens are young threes," she replied. "We consider two point nine to be more of an 'old two.'" In other words, Connor was entering this process with one strike already against him: my subpar choice of conception date.

For preschools in Manhattan, the best birthdays are September to November. Dates from December to February are "not ideal," March to May are "less than optimal," and if you have a summer baby, it's time to consider home schooling. Manhattan moms in the know plan their conceptions to occur sometime just after Chinese New Year, so that their children will have an ultra-desirable autumn birthday. Like I said, I'm from Scranton, so I didn't know about that. This meant that Connor was an "old two," so close and yet so far from the "young three" crowd, and we walked out of the Meaningful Montessori of Manhattan knowing Connor would probably not be invited to join their school community.

I was not worried. That just proved my prudence in applying to a variety of options. I would never have been so foolish as to put all my eggs on the Montessori play mat. Why, the Hudson International Children's School had a room specifically designated for "old twos"! Three days later, with a renewed sense of optimism, David and I arrived at Hudson International for a group tour.

This school was a renovated former church. It had soaring ceilings that were lovely to look at but also considerably amplified the din of seven classrooms' worth of preschoolers discussing the letter of the week at top volume. We were shown to the art gallery with about six other sets of parents while we waited. Various finger-painted and macaroni-glued creations were hung there, neatly framed and lit from above. While David immersed himself in his BlackBerry, trying to keep his job despite missing yet another Tuesday-morning sales meeting, I perused the artwork and sussed out the competition. I had finally figured out the proper uniform for a nursery school appearance: lightweight wool trousers, jewel-toned cashmere sweater, and shoes with a heel. I had also bought a grown-up purse to sling over my shoulder instead of the black vinyl diaper bag I normally used, the one they give away for free on maternity wards. Not too much jewelry, but some. Not too much makeup, but some. I had succeeded on all these fronts. But my God, when did all these other mothers have time to flat-iron their hair?

At 9:05 A.M., a petite woman swept dramatically into the room. "Good morning, parents, and welcome to the nut-and-seed-free Hudson International Children's School!" she said in a pan-European accent. "I am Daphne Divakaruni, Hudson International's admissions coordinator." Ms. Divakaruni said this last part humbly, as if she quite obviously needed no such introduction. She wore a kente cloth scarf around her neck, draped in an Isadora Duncan–goes-on-safari way. It signaled that she was a freethinking sort of educator. "I am confident that you will find in our school a uniquely enriched, teacher-led curriculum for your two-to-four-year-old," she intoned. "Our educational approach encompasses the best of the HighScope and Reggio Emilia philosophies, with which I am sure you are already familiar."

Half a dozen mothers and a few fathers nodded enthusiastically. "What the hell is she talking about?" David muttered, pocketing his BlackBerry with some resentment. I gave him the evil eye: cooperate or die.

Ms. Divakaruni led our tour group down the hallway, calling over her shoulder as she went. "The first classroom you will see is our medium threes, whom we like to call the 'Steam Locomotives.'" She stopped us at the doorway. "Take a peek inside. You may smile at the Steam Locomotives, but please do not speak to them; they are currently finishing their unit on Vincent van Gogh, and we do not want to disturb them." We peeked at fourteen three-year-olds, hard at work on Post-Impressionist landscapes. "What nice work, Steam Locomotives!" Ms. Divakaruni crowed as we departed.

After looking at Hudson's computer lab, ceramics room, woodworking shop, and pottery kiln, we came to the kitchen. "If you peek in here," Ms. Divakaruni cooed, "you will see our old twos, who we call the 'Endangered Species of the Rain Forest,' creating assorted sweetmeats for the upcoming festival of Diwali. I think I speak for everyone when I say, good job, Endangered Species of the Rain Forest!" The other parents murmured their assent.

By now Ms. Divakaruni had brought us in a full circle back to the art gallery, where she delivered her stirring conclusion. "As you can plainly see, no activity is done lightly at the Hudson International Children's School. When our children have music class, they may skip and jump, but always with a rhythm, a cadence. When they play in the sandbox, we offer conversational scripts for the children to practice conflict resolution. When they listen to a story, it is always in Mandarin Chinese. At the Hudson International Children's School, we take our fun *very*. Seriously."

"I'm not sure that Connor *needs* a pottery kiln," David said that evening, toothbrush in hand. "Let alone Mandarin Chinese story time."

"That is not the point!" I replied. "We need to be worried about him getting *in,* not about whether some school's hydroponic gardens mesh with our personal educational goals."

"Stop worrying," David said, twisting floss around his finger. "As soon as they meet Connor, they're gonna love him. He'll get in everywhere."

Maybe David was right. Connor was adorable and brilliant, and his parents were only a wee bit biased. Even if my mothering skills—and his conception date—were substandard, once these admissions directors actually met Connor, his bright, talkative self would beguile the hell out of them. And Connor's turn in the spotlight had come.

The final portion of the application process was what each school casually called a "playdate" or "visit." These were, ostensibly, opportunities for the wee applicants to see the school, play with a few toys, and allow the admissions committee to place faces with names. But by now, the scales had fallen from my eyes. I knew that as soon as we entered each school, everything Connor did would be ranked on his scorecard. And mine.

For Connor's "playdate" at West End Christian Country Day, I pomaded his cowlick into submission and dressed him in his absolutely irresistible roll-neck monogrammed sweater.

(For this round, it was acceptable for only one parent to be present, and David was thrilled to be back at work.) We walked to WECCD but stopped a block away so I could get Connor out of the stroller; I had heard that the schools cast an approving eye on not-quite-two-year-olds who walked in by themselves. I then resorted to promises of lollipops and "wonderful prizes" in order to confiscate Connor's pacifier without tears. When *my* toddler entered West End Christian Country Day, he would be on his own two feet, unplugged, and perhaps even smiling.

We were greeted in the school's lobby with the other children and parents, and escorted as a group to the test site: a nursery classroom, unoccupied except for three or four female administrators standing around with clipboards. They nodded to us without speaking and gestured to little tables, neatly arranged with plastic animals and glue sticks and homemade Play-Doh. Here was . . .

Toddler Test Number One: Separation.

Our children were supposed to quickly and neatly separate from us parents and play happily in the classroom while we stood along the wall, remaining uninvolved. Successful separation would be a major sign of Connor's readiness for school nine months hence, but was in direct contradiction to the "Stay right with Mommy!" advice he usually got a hundred times a day or so. I pried Connor's hands off my leg and crouched down to his level. "Ooh, honey, look!" I said, eyes popping out of my head in mock delight. "Little animals! Your favorite! Go play!" Connor looked at them, then back at me, a little unsure. "Yes, you go play!" I said, with animation bordering on the mad. "Connor goes and plays, and Mommy's going to be *right there!*" I pointed to the wall, a tantalizing five feet away.

Connor didn't move. Most of the parents had successfully separated already. Seats at the little animals table were rapidly dwindling. One of the ladies with the clipboards was watching. I backed away slowly, maintaining eye contact, repeating this calming mantra: "You're over there, and I'm right here, and you're right there, and Mommy's right—here!" My butt touched wall. Connor turned away and picked up some plastic animals. I nearly wet my pants with relief. Then I nodded and smiled pleasantly at the other parents, and gave an I-been-there-sister! rueful glance to the mother whose kid had broken into full sobbing at the mere suggestion of their sundering. I saw the admissions director make a clandestine mark on her clipboard. Ding. *That* kid was not getting in.

I am ashamed to say that I gloated at this. I did feel sorry for this mother, who was saying, "Ha ha! He's not usually like this! Uh ha ha ha!" in a tone that belied her extreme agitation. On the other hand, every kid who *wasn't* crying could, at that moment, have been taking Connor's spot. I mean, there was one kid in black knee socks who was sniffing the markers, but I overheard his mother saying they were French Canadian, so he was probably a shoo-in. In this world, it was every toddler for himself.

The administrators worked the room, observing our children at play, making notes here and there on their clipboards. "I like your sweater!" the head teacher said to Connor. *Say "thank you,"* I prayed. Instead he regarded her solemnly, plastic animals clenched in each fist. The admissions director saw this little standoff and approached. I held my breath.

"Hello . . . 'Connor.' What a nice giraffe you have there."

He stared at both of them.

"Can you tell me what he says?"

Connor looked at her, mouth open, saying nothing. The admissions director moved on to a grouping at the Play-Doh table. Connor had failed . . .

Toddler Test Number Two: The Answering of the Grown-Up's Question That Is Very Confusing and Yet Must Be Answered.

I wanted to chase after this admissions director and clarify for her that (1) it had been a trick question, since a giraffe doesn't say *anything,* and (2) Connor, in a familiar environment, was an extremely expressive communicator for his age group. But under no circumstances was I supposed to leave my spot along the wall. I was there strictly to observe. I chewed my lip instead.

"Snack time, children!" the head teacher called. Connor took his tiny seat without further invitation and waited brilliantly with the other children. Then he and I were both blindsided by . . .

Toddler Test Number Three: The Dixie Cup of Water.

A wobbly, wet paper cup of water was set in front of Connor as aperitif. My God, I had never seen this coming. Connor *hated* water! He only drank juice. Watered down, of course. But what if he spoke up and said so? Even worse, he had never drunk out of a real cup—I only gave him sippy cups at home! How could I have been so stupid? Of course his hand-eye coordination and healthy hydration skills were going to be assessed! Connor took a tentative sip, holding the already disintegrating paper cup in both hands. I could hardly even watch. *Don't spill don't spill don't spill,* I begged silently.

Then the tests came faster and faster, each evaluating skills I had not actually taught my toddler yet, me digging half moons into my palms with my fingernails:

The Graham Crackers Test.

Don't stuff! I shrieked inwardly. *No crumbs! No, not your sleeve! The napkin!*

The Sitting Nicely Until Everyone Else Is Done Test.

Connor started to climb off his chair, and I attempted to mind-meld him from across the room: *Sit! SIT!* By now, I had full underarm stains from the incapacitation.

And that was when the director of admissions said: "Now we have time for a few minutes of free play before we sing our good-bye song." Free play! As in, completely unstructured activity! There was no way to screw that up. We were almost home.

Connor looked around him, one finger up his nose, discerning what most deserved his attention in these final moments. Was it the easel? The sand table? He surveyed all his choices and decided that in a classroom with eight thousand options, what he really needed was the dump truck the boy in the black knee socks was playing with.

Connor tugged at the truck. The boy tugged back. Back and forth they pulled. Back. Forth. *"C'est le mien!"* Knee

Socks Boy cried, and Connor got that look on his face, that "Hulk mad" look, and did I mention he was an occasional biter? If I left the wall, I would destroy the cardinal rule of the preschool playdate. If I stayed there, Connor would take a chunk out of his adversary's arm. I saw Connor's nursery school career flash before my eyes, and so I ran over, calling, "Hey! Hey! Hey! Honey, are we sharing? 'Cause you know how to share!" Connor and Knee Socks Boy continued their tug-of-war. "Now, you are going to share with this nice little boy!" I said, raising my voice despite my attempt to remain cheerful. "Share with him! Share! For the love of God, *SHARE!*"

The room had gone silent. Seventeen pairs of eyes regarded me, on the floor, shouting and wrestling with my son for a dump truck (Knee Socks Boy had dropped the truck in abject fear several moments earlier). The admissions director made a mark on her clipboard. Ding.

Fine. I had gone a little overboard. Maybe I should have let Connor bite. I learned my lesson, and at all the other playdates stayed against the wall with arms folded. With each school we visited, Connor's confidence with Dixie cups and sewing cards grew. He understood what we were there for and acted with a maturity far beyond his years (with the tacit understanding he would get his pacifier back as soon as we were outside). He said please and thank you, he didn't cry, and at the Creativity Circle School, he bused his *own juice box* after snack time. What more could they want from a two-year-old?

We would only have to wait until spring to find out. After a few months' worth of second-guessing our application essays and listing the preschools in our order of preference, the first Tuesday in March arrived at last. Nine letters from nine preschools arrived in that afternoon's mail. I plopped Connor in front of Nick Jr. and opened the letters with trembling hands.

> *We were very fortunate to meet such interesting parents and captivating children during this application season. Our visit with Connor was a delight, and we are sad not to be able to offer him a space at this time.*

> *We have placed Connor on our waiting list. We will contact you in the event that an opening occurs.*

> *We are delighted to offer Connor a place—on our Waiting List.*

> *We are offering Connor a place on our PRIORITY waiting list.*

> *We are sorry to say we do not have a spot for Connor.*

They didn't sound very sorry to me. Whether they couched it in nice terms or not, the first eight letters all said the same thing: we are rejecting your child.

I swallowed, trying to stem the tide of terror rising in my chest. I had known that getting completely shut out was a distinct possibility. I had heard stories, told in hushed tones, of a child's not getting in anywhere at all, the whole family having to move away in shame to someplace where nursery schools were less selective. Until now, though, I had never really believed it could happen to Connor. To us. What were we going to do?

There was only one letter left. I was almost too afraid to open it, but I had to know the worst. On a single typed page with rainbow letterhead, it said,

> *I am pleased to inform you that Connor has been accepted as an "Endangered Species of the Rain Forest" at Hudson International Children's School. Welcome, Connor!*
>
> *Warmly,*
> *Daphne Divakaruni*

Here was one bit of good news: we did not have to agonize over choosing the "right" school for Connor. He only got into one school out of nine.

That was all we needed, wasn't it? My goal had been to get him in somewhere, and we had, and Hudson International was actually pretty good. I understood going in that these nursery schools snubbed most of their applicants. That one shouldn't take it personally. Why was it still so devastating?

Because this application process had been the litmus test of everything I had done for Connor so far. And based on the results, I'd done a shitty job. One out of *nine*? Where had I gone so totally, completely wrong that eight schools could see it? This couldn't have been Connor's fault. Well, except the school where he bit. The rest of it was all me. With eight rejections but no explanations, I conjured up my own lengthy list of possibilities, all pointing to my evident shortcomings as a parent.

My husband saw no need for further reflection. "Let it go," David said. "He has a spot. Everything is fine. Let it go." And he was right, of course. That fall, Connor played with blocks three mornings a week at the Hudson International Children's School, and even though he cried when I left every morning until Thanksgiving, he loved it. Even the pottery kiln.

I wish I could say that in the end, I learned how silly and inconsequential the whole process was. But I remained stung by the rejection, and I wondered, for a long time, how I might have done things differently. I'm still not sure there is anything I could have changed. That does not really make me feel better. While I can roll my eyes at what I had to do to get Connor a cubby in the cloakroom, I cannot say, even today, that I have ever felt my efforts were unnecessary. On that day in March, as I held those nursery school letters in my hand, my main takeaway was this bone-deep certainty: my children were all going to have disappointments in their lives. When those times came, it might be only a small comfort to understand, as I now did, that whatever it was that happened, it would be completely and absolutely Mommy's fault.

CHAPTER TEN

A Tale of Two Mommies

Now that I am an old lady, my idea of a perfect evening no longer includes dinner in a cloth-napkin restaurant and dancing 'til two. These days, a great night for me occurs when David is out at some work dinner and my kids all go to sleep more or less on time. On such an enchanted evening, I settle eagerly into the couch with my laptop, my inbox of nearly overdue bills, a glass of oaky chardonnay, the remote control, and The Learning Channel, the cable network featuring toddlers in tiaras, women who didn't know they were pregnant, and families notable for their improbable number of children.

What always gets me about these shows is how eerily tranquil these enormous households all seem. Every episode is set up like, "uh-oh, we're going to take the sextuplets to the dentist, *this* should be interesting . . ." and then it's calm and measured and totally fine. Heaven knows these mothers have all had their issues, but they are usually with travel logistics, or no-good husbands, or the lack of privacy for which they can really only blame themselves. These mothers are not tearing their hair out as their passels of children run wild. Taking care of the children seems to be the easy part, and I can't say I am as composed, ever, as these mothers of multitudes are, always. Even if David or the babysitter or my mom is around to help—or, for that matter, all of them—my kids want "only Mommy" to cut their meat or wash their hiney or whatever; and the din of their concurrent needs being shouted above the buzz of the dishwasher I neglected to turn on that morning does get to me.

On TV at least, these families-cum–day care centers never seem as loud as my household. They never seem loud at all. And if one of the little rascals should have a difficult moment, his mother will always handle it with great reserves of patience and grace. I remember one show in which a fresh-scrubbed, Jesus-loving lad of about eight was having a tantrum. I cannot recall his exact grounds for rebellion; "I don't want to wear long underwear under my clothes, it's July," he was perhaps saying. His mother knelt down to his level as he carried on, made loving eye contact with him, and said, "Jebediah. Jebediah, sweetheart, look at Mommy." She was speaking so quietly he couldn't hear her and cry at the same time. Jebediah stopped and gazed at his mother.

"Sweetheart," she continued at her subsonic frequency, "why are you not doing what I am asking you to do? Because I know you know how to do it. You are a big boy." That was all it took. Jebediah wiped away his own tears and donned his woolen union suit without further incident. Like I said, I'm a little fuzzy on the details—it might have been a hair shirt, size 4T—but it was the overall effectiveness of this mother's disciplinary approach that struck me. Without raising her voice, indeed by lowering it, she defused her son's tantrum quickly and peacefully.

I saw this episode at some point when Seamus's Year of Being Completely Intractable had just begun, right before his fourth birthday. The next evening, as he raged against bedtime, though clearly exhausted, and started to kick me while his baby sister screamed for me from her crib down the hall, I tried a little tenderness. I pinned him down with my body as he screamed, madly scissoring his little legs. Then I murmured in his ear: "Sweetheart, did you know? There is a Good Seamus who lives on this shoulder, right here. And on this shoulder, over here, lives Bold Seamus."

Here, a clarification. Whenever I misbehaved as a child, my mother would always scold me for being a "bold" girl. Never "bad" or "naughty." I thought all mothers had "bold" in their repertoire until I had a child old enough to discipline and started getting weird looks at playgroup. I have since discovered by perusing the dictionary that "bold" is part of my ethnic heritage:

> **bold** (adjective)
> 1 showing an ability to take risks; confident and courageous
> 2 having a strong or vivid appearance
> 3 (of a cliff or coast) steep or projecting
> 4 Irish (of a child) naughty; badly behaved

These days I seem to be the only parent at the playground who uses "bold" in the fourth sense of the word. Most mothers are more likely to apply the term to a craggy coastline than to their own children. But I like it. "Bold" gets your point across without your having to scar your kids forever with a "bad" diagnosis. When my mother called me "bold," I knew

I had to get my act together, but I didn't think she hated me or anything. And "bold" was as severe as she ever got. If I had hot-wired a car during my teen years, my mother might have deemed me "bad," but now I'll never know.

During one of Seamus's recent tantrums, he had put me in my place by calling me "a bold mommy *and* a bad mommy." I had not yet stooped to that level of insult, though heaven knows it would have been an accurate assessment. But Seamus was termed "bold" several times each day, and if Seamus was surprised there were mini-hims living on his shoulders, I'm sure he was mostly shocked that one of them was "good."

He stopped kicking his legs in the bed, his little chest heaving with suppressed sobs so he could hear what I was whispering in his ear. "The good Seamus and the bold Seamus both tell you what you should be doing. And it's hard to know which one to listen to sometimes, isn't it?"

"Wait. Dere are wittle *me's* on my *solders*?" Seamus breathed, craning his neck from side to side. "Do you *see* dem, for weal weal wife?"

"I certainly do," I answered.

"Why don't I see dem?" he whispered.

"Because they like to hide in your ears," I said, countering. His eyes grew wide.

At this point, I had drifted considerably from the original concept. It's supposed to be an angel and a devil on your shoulders, not tiny versions of yourself, although I definitely recall a *Tom and Jerry* episode where Tom had two teeny gray cats on his shoulders, one wielding a pitchfork. But for something I had made up on the fly, it wasn't bad, and Seamus was very taken with the idea. "What are dey saying?" he whispered, listening hard but hearing nothing.

"Well," I vamped, very proud of myself, "Bold Seamus is saying, 'Kick Mommy! Kick her again! I don't want to go to sleep!' and Good Seamus is saying, 'Oh, but I sure do. I sure am tired.'"

And gosh-darn it, Seamus the Good lay down and went to sleep, and for the next several days, his tantrums ebbed nicely. He had a far-off look in his eyes as he listened intently for the next missive from his tiny conscience companions. "What is Bold Seamus saying *wight now*?" he'd ask. He was always more interested in what Bold Seamus was saying, and really, who wouldn't be? But merely talking about Bold Seamus, the Lord of Misrule, had become as satisfying as any actual misbehavior. "Bold Seamus want to bweak Connor's bwock stwucture!" Seamus would roar, and then could be calmly redirected without his actually doing it. I considered myself a parenting genius for two full weeks, until suddenly any mention of what Bold Seamus was thinking or doing was enough to summon him from the underworld for a week's stay or longer, and the whole line of discussion had to be dropped entirely.

By a few months later, I had forgotten all about it. I was giving Connor his five weekly minutes of quality Mommy time, hanging out on the toilet seat while he took his bath. "Mommy," Connor said, attempting to float on his back in our tub, which was quickly becoming too small for him to lie down in, "Mommy, do you remember how there are two Seamuses?"

"Oh. Sure I do, bud."

"Well, did you know there are also two Mommies?"

"Really?" I said, smiling indulgently as I imagined what six-year-old bon mot might issue from his lips. "Who are they?"

"Well, there's the nice Mommy, and—"

"And?"

"—and, the—other one," he said, closing his eyes and dipping his ears below the surface of the water, giving me a moment perched on the toilet seat to take this all in.

There *are* two of me. One of me swings my two sons' hands as we stroll three abreast to the corner to wait for the bus in the morning. We all have the same smile.

Then there is the other me, the one who storms into her sons' room the next morning, saying, "How many times do I have to tell you to put your *G-D shoes on* we are going to *MISS THE BUS!*" and sees, just for a moment, their fear that one of those shoes might be winged at them.

I have never thrown shoes at my children. But I have thrown shoes at the wall. I have grabbed my boys by the scruffs of their shirts and deposited them in their Time Out chairs with more force then was perhaps necessary. I have even spanked their behinds, once for biting another kid, and a few other times for things that seemed really awful at the moment, but which can't have been as bad as they seemed, since I can no longer recall what they even were. Most egregiously, however, I am a yeller. At least once a week, I will hear one of my children scream from the other end of the house, an unholy wail, and when I swoop in and see the truck in one son's hand and the rapidly rising welt on the other son's face, I will Lose My Shit. If I am not a Bad Mommy at times like this, I am certainly a very, very Bold One.

Of course, I always apologize as soon as I calm down, and give my kids a hug, and since thirty seconds later they're playing together again, untroubled by it all, I have assumed that making proper amends at least separates me from the really rotten apples. Sitting there watching Connor hold his breath under the water, though, I realized that saying you're sorry for having been a jerk is not really as powerful an example for your children as not having been a jerk in the first place.

At least Connor had said there were two of me, which, loosely interpreted, meant I was sometimes *not* horrible to be around. And as my friend Missy pointed out, I couldn't be *that* scary a mommy if Connor felt okay bringing it up in the first place. But he had brought it up. I did not want my children to grow up being scared of me, even once in a while, so I needed to make some changes. I bought an armful of books with jaunty, self-actualizing titles like *Parenting in Peace-s* and *Keep It Down!* Most of these books spent the first two-thirds of their pages telling me how Really Important it was that I stop yelling at my children. This seemed like a colossal waste of ink; if I thought yelling at my kids was fine and dandy, sirs, I would not be reading your books. Plus, I can only read three pages a night before falling asleep, so couldn't they just get to the point already? After a few weeks of these books on my bedside table, I had at least assimilated their overall message: Children look to parents for consistency. If you show them that you can remain in control, so, eventually, will they.

Well, if all I had to do to have well-behaved children was to be well-behaved myself, I was ready to begin. When the boys came to blows at the breakfast table the next morning over who liked Cinnamon Life more, I tried one of my new Mellow Mommy lines on them:

"Whoa, sounds like both of you are a little steamed."

And I said it in this totally relaxed, quiet voice, too. Wasn't that good? I was reflecting their feelings without judgment.

The only problem was, neither of them could hear me, because Connor was screeching so loudly the veins in his neck were standing out: "I! Like! Cinnamon! Life! *The! MOST!*"

"That sure is an angry message," I said, still trying what the books had assured me would work. "Seamus, would you like to respond?" At which point, Bold Seamus apparently whispered in Real Seamus's ear that he should dump his beloved Cinnamon Life on his brother's head.

I ask you: would this not have been too much, even for the SuperNanny? I went apoplectic on the two of them: "Why can't you just *get along* for *five minutes!*" But as I rounded the corner from that tirade into the "Food is not for wasting" harangue, I stopped short. The two boys, instead of looking at me, or at least looking down in abject shame, were regarding each other across the kitchen table, Connor with Cinnamon Life still in his hair. They were both smirking.

It was one thing to go banshee on my children and at least feel that it was, as a medium-to-last resort, successful behavioral modification. But if they could snicker at my yelling? If they had gotten *used* to it? That was even more reason to stop. If I were forced to defend myself under subpoena, like Jack Bauer on *24*, I would be forced to admit that not only was I a Bold Mommy, but that my "enhanced compliance techniques" hadn't even worked.

I stepped up my non-yelling efforts. I gave yelling up for Lent instead of caffeine. I was not entirely successful in abstaining, but when I did get the urge to yell for those forty days, I thought: *Well, I hope this hollering will really be worth it, since you are breaking a promise to your family that you made before God.* Usually, by the time I had finished thinking all that, the kids would be on to something else anyhow.

There are certainly times when a good lung workout is called for—say, when Seamus is about to scooter into the path of a FedEx truck—but that is all the more reason to save the screaming for when I really need it. The hardest part is recognizing, in the moment, that my kid having the effrontery to whine "I didn't say I wanted peanut butter with *grape* jelly" is not an instance where utterly losing my mind is really warranted. It is a moment to listen to Good Mommy, to do the exact opposite of what my baser instincts are telling me: lower my voice instead of raise it, model flexibility rather than impatience, embrace my child rather than my frustration. I can say that I yell less than I used to. But I still have a long way to go.

One day last month, my friend Cece gave Connor and me a ride home from his school after pickup. Her two boys, strapped a little too closely together in their booster seats (how else was she supposed to fit their little sister's humongo Britax Roundabout in the same row?) started screeching at each other about who was the rightful owner of a LEGO piece so small it was barely visible to the naked eye. The two of them screamed for the rest of the ride at a level distressing enough to trigger embolism. I looked over at Cece to gauge her reaction. Gripping the steering wheel with white knuckles, she drove the whole way to our house, staring straight ahead, without making any attempt to stop their caterwauling. I couldn't believe she wasn't going ballistic. How could she keep it together and *drive,* for Pete's sake, with that going on in the backseat? I figured I would never be as patient as Cece.

Then, that evening, an e-mail. "Sorry about today," Cece wrote. "As soon as you got out of the car, I became the most horrible mother in the world. I've never screamed at the kids like that. I just didn't want you and Connor to see it." Little did she know how much I wished I had. It was quite comforting to imagine my calm and centered friend with her eyes bulging from their sockets. Perhaps there are two mommies in all of us, even in TLC's selfless, home-schooling mother of nineteen, and it will certainly make for compelling viewing if we ever get to witness *her* dark side.

As for me, I cannot deny that Bold Mommy is there on my shoulder, just waiting for her chance to reemerge. My children know it too. When Bold Mommy tells me to fly off the handle, and I struggle mightily to keep it together, I still see a flicker of worry in Connor's eyes: is Mommy about to be scary? Usually, that is all the reminder I need to stay on the Good Mommy side; a mother should, above all, make her children feel safe. Perhaps one day, if Bold Mommy doesn't show her face for a long, long time, my kids might forget about her. Until then, the best I can do is show them that when Bold Mommy whispers in my ear, I hear her. But I choose not to listen.

CHAPTER ELEVEN

The Big P

It was 6:45 P.M., and Connor the Kindergartner had started his nightly refrain:

> **CONNOR:** I don't want to take a bath.
> **ME:** You have to take a bath.
> **CONNOR:** I took one last night!
> **ME:** No, you didn't.

Connor sighed heavily as he walked down the hallway, off to the gallows.

> **CONNOR:** Can it be a *short* bath, at least?
> **ME:** Fine. Just wash face, hands, feet, and . . .

I pointed to the below-the-belt areas, fore and aft.

I'm not sure why I did this. I could have simply said "penis" and "hiney," as we say every day in our house.

(Granted, "hiney" is not anatomically correct, but I think saying "Let Mommy wipe your buttocks" is just *too* silly.) I think that when I gestured to Connor's penis and hiney, rather than naming them, I was reflecting Connor's recent and sudden privacy concerning his private parts. He now wanted to wash those parts of himself *by* himself, rather than have me do it for him, as I had every night until a week or so before. Connor had a new understanding that his penis and, say, his elbow were not to be treated with equal casualness. So I did my little mime, then said,

ME: Wash all of that, and you can get out, buddy.

and walked down the hall to pull out his pajamas. After ninety seconds or so, Connor yelled,

CONNOR: Mom! I'm done!
ME: Okay, honey!

And as I walked back down the hall to the bathroom:

CONNOR: I washed my wiener hole!

This was one of those moments when you are just so, so sorry to be the only adult present. I popped my head around the bathroom door.

ME: Your what?
CONNOR: I washed my wiener, and my wiener hole.

I bit the inside of my cheek, hard. Laughing would shatter

the magic of the moment. This called for some Mommy Mock Horror, a move perfected by my own mother.

> **ME:** Connor! Where did you hear words like that?
> **CONNOR:** At school.
> **ME:** Those are not words we use in this house.
> **CONNOR:** (confused) But, Mommy. It's politer to say "wiener" than "penis."
> **ME:** What? No, it's not.
> **CONNOR:** (quite sure) Yes, it is.

Now I was the one who was confused. Is it politer to say "wiener" than "penis"? Under certain circumstances, I supposed perhaps it was. And what about "wee wee"? Was that the terminology best used when at, say, a high tea? I was no longer sure about any of it, and I therefore proceeded with caution.

> **ME:** Well. If you're trying to be really polite, it's better not to say either one of those words. But if you're in science class, and you're talking about your body, it's okay to say "penis." And if you're having hot dogs for lunch, it's okay to say "wiener."
> **CONNOR:** Why?
> **ME:** Well—because—a hot dog *is* a wiener. That's what a wiener is.

Connor's jaw dropped.

> **CONNOR:** WIENER MEANS HOT DOG?

And then he laughed for the next fifteen minutes. Eventually I had to just leave him in there while he yelled down the hall, "Mommy! I washed my hot dog!" and other such repartee, another sign my little boy was becoming the grown-up sort of little boy.

Soon after that, Connor announced that he was forgoing baths entirely and would henceforth take only showers. "Please, Mom, do *not come in!*" he would shriek if I cracked the bathroom door to check on him. "I'm make-id in here!" A week after that, as part of a teary afternoon where he told me he "just felt sad for no reason," Connor emerged from his bedroom, crayon in hand.

CONNOR: How do you spell "away"?
ME: A-W-
CONNOR: Don't tell me how to spell "go," though, I know that.
ME: Why do you want to write "Go away"?

Connor held up two pieces of construction paper, one red and one green.

CONNOR: I'm making two signs for my door. The red one will say "Go Away," and if you see it, you can't come in my room. The green one will say "Go Ahead," and that means you can come in if you want to, if you knock first and say, "Can I come in?" and I say, "Go ahead."

I explained to Connor that while we would all respect

his privacy, he shared a room with his younger brother, and so there would be times when Seamus would have to come in even if the red sign were posted. Seamus looked up from where he was playing on the floor nearby with his Walkin' Talkin' Lightning McQueen.

> **SEAMUS:** That's okay, Mommy. I don't fink I have to go in.
> **ME:** You don't have to go in your own room?
> **SEAMUS:** Nope.
> **ME:** Ever?

Seamus just shrugged.

There I was, with two sons: a six-year-old who suddenly craved extreme privacy, and another, a year and a half younger, who couldn't imagine why he'd ever want a moment to himself. Seamus is a "before" picture of blissful ignorance, and he takes care of his personal business no matter who is watching. For Seamus, there is nothing finer than watching *Wacky Races* on the couch in his jammies with elasticized waistband, all the better to get both hands down his pants at the same time. He has no hang-ups about this whatsoever. I try not to either, but one night I couldn't help myself and said,

> **ME:** Shea, it's not really nice to do that.
> **SEAMUS:** Do what?
> **ME:** Uh. Touch your penis like that in the middle of the living room.

Seamus looked at me like I was an idiot.

SEAMUS: Mommy. I'm zust playin' Cut the Cucumber.

He then gave me a most un-self-conscious demonstration of said game and its rather free-form rules.

Seamus loves his body. To my mind, he is a bit *too* comfortable with it, but in consideration of the healthy adult male I wish to create, I try to be largely nonjudgmental about how often he plays Cut the Cucumber, as long as he is doing it more or less in private. One recent morning, though, he started being brazen with himself while we all stood on the street corner waiting for the bus. "Seamus," I said, "honey, you can do that at home in your bed if you'd like, but you can't do that in public," trying to, as the books would tell me, redirect without shame.

"What's a pubwic?" Seamus asked.

"Yeah, Mom," Connor asked, piping in as if he had been waiting for the right moment to bring this up, "what's a public?" There we stood at the bus stop while I explained the notions of public, private, and masturbation itself, a talk I had been expecting to have, oh, some time *after* pre-K. I explained that while touching yourself was a wonderful and *totally normal* means of self-expression, it was something best done in the privacy of your room. How modern was I! No judgment, none of my own sexual issues being visited upon my offspring. But Seamus was staring at me blankly, hands still down his pants, and I felt like I was giving Connor, who had never considered such behavior, an intriguing new reason to put the red "Go Away" sign up on his door.

With years left to go before my children enter puberty, I am already navigating tricky waters. I am never sure where on the prude/hippie spectrum I am supposed to be, either for their good or for mine. For example, my kids still see me naked. This is not well thought out on my part; it happens less by design than necessity. If both boys are on my bed by 6:30 A.M., watching cartoons while I shower, and if Maggie decides to spend those few moments of my stolen freedom with her hands splayed against the steamy glass door, her mouth O'd wide like a ghost desperate to escape from the spirit world, she gets a good look at me in the altogether. And then when I get out, and Connor and Seamus start a face-scratching competition before my underwear is on, they too may see my saggy bare ass when I intervene.

David has suggested that our children, especially Connor, should probably stop seeing me naked at some point in the near future. And I fully intend to bring it to a close, just as soon as I can trust my kids to not kill each other for a full four minutes. When's that, twelfth grade? Until then, well, they've all had my boob in their mouth a thousand times, whether or not they are currently consciously aware of that, and it no longer seems like I have much to be modest about. This goes for everyone. I live in the middle of New York City, and sometimes I don't even bother to close my curtains before I get dressed. Honestly, if you want to take a look, go for it. I'm no longer excited enough about my body to feel proprietary.

Sometimes I think it's good for my children to see what a mother of three's body looks like in real life, so that their standards will remain realistic. But have I already exceeded the appropriate deadline for nude mommies? It's kind of like how you have to breastfeed your baby until he's a year, or else you're a bad mother; but if you breastfeed a single day *past* the one-year mark, that's gross and there's something wrong with you. The window is extremely narrow, and am I a bad mother for having perhaps missed it entirely? Maybe I am excessively Bohemian in this regard. I think it's because, breastfeeding all three of them, I got used to being at least half naked at least half of the time. In contrast, I was bottle-fed, and I don't think I saw my own mother naked, ever. All my life, she has been the patron saint of modesty. Have I grown up to be a less warped adult for it?

And how old do Seamus and Maggie have to be before they stop bathing together? Despite its efficiency, I fear that too is drawing to a close. Just last week, Seamus decided to fully recline in the bathtub. His little penis bobbed to the surface of the water. With much curiosity, Maggie put aside her rubber duckie to have a closer look-see at this new bath toy. Seamus saw her coming but made no attempt to correct the situation. On the contrary, he crossed his arms behind his head, like a caricature of a satisfied, stogie-smoking politician. Let's just say I quickly intervened.

ME: Seamus, your penis is just for you.
SEAMUS: Why?

Well, that was a good question. Was a four-year-old ready to hear me say, "Well. It's just for you, or, once you reach sexual maturity, other romantic partners, of indeterminate gender, with whom you are in a consensual relationship"? I decided against it.

ME: Because it's your private place.
SEAMUS: Why?

ME: Christ on a stick, Seamus, get out of the bathtub!

I really should plan ahead for such moments. I need to have three different age-appropriate birds-and-bees speeches, one for each child, memorized and ready to go at all times. I am procrastinating in doing this, because I would really rather not have these talks at all. My mother never told me the facts of life. Of course, she didn't really need to, since Judy Blume's *Forever* was being passed under the desks by fifth grade. But I'm pretty sure I was not full of questions to make my mother uncomfortable when I was in *kindergarten,* and even if I was, I'm sure she deflected them with great skill.

I do not have my mother's subject-changing power, and by attempting to give my children information that is user-friendly and reassuring, I am forever painting myself into corners. I have told my boys in the past that babies come from a mommy and daddy giving each other a special hug and praying to God to put a baby in the mommy's tummy. This worked well, until Connor recently asked me:

CONNOR: Mommy, why is it rare for a horse to be all white?
ME: Well. They have to be bred that way. You need a white mommy horse *and* a white daddy horse to make a white baby horse.
CONNOR: But . . . how *do* they?

I didn't see where he was headed.

ME: How do they what?

CONNOR: Horses can't pray.
ME: . . . No . . .
CONNOR: So who prays for the white baby horse to be in the mother horse's tummy? Is it the farmer?

My "special hug and a prayer" story is taking on water faster than I can bail. Since the white horse quiz, Connor has also asked me if, when his classmate Lucy's two daddies did *their* special hug, they had to pray for Lucy to be in another mommy's tummy, and if so, how did God know which lady to pick? I said (1) yes, and (2) the daddies made sure to *tell* God which lady in their prayer. (One would want to be pretty specific with that request.) I hope I bought myself some time. I am somewhat relieved that I may have to explain to Connor the logistics of surrogate mothers and in vitro fertilization long before I actually explain what men like to do with their wieners.

Even so, I try to put it all off. When Connor's questions get too tricky for me, I tell him that I will get him a book to answer all of his questions. Then, I do not. Assuming there is an age-appropriate book I can read to Connor with a straight face, I really should get it. Alternatively, I could tell him to go ask his father. But Connor's asking me, and I know I won't always have that privilege. If my son is looking to me for answers, the burden rests on my shoulders. If I am to be the honest and trustworthy mother that I want to be to my children, there are a lot of discussions of uncomfortable topics ahead. With each of my children, I will have to find the right language to discuss them. I cannot say I am looking forward to those conversations, especially (heaven help me) with my daughter. But those days are coming, and they will not be delayed just because I think it's too soon.

In the meantime, Connor has intuited that his body is changing, and it is ironic that his need for privacy has come at the same moment he has grown so amazing to behold. He looks a little taller to me every morning. He is sinewy and lithe and almost-seven, and on his sturdy chest are written all the wonderful things he might become. He is all possibility, a bud, and when I watch him take a running jump into the swimming pool, I wonder how that strapping youngster ever fit inside me. No wonder I'm so stretched out.

Last night, after his shower, Connor stuck his head in the kitchen.

CONNOR: I washed everything, Mom.
ME: Sounds good.
CONNOR: I washed the Big P and the Big B.

I nodded, biting the inside of my cheek again.

ME: Is that what we're going to call them now?
CONNOR: I think so. I think it's politer.
ME: Okay, then. Why "Big P," though? Why not just "The P"?
CONNOR: Well, I thought about that. But then I thought it would be confusing. A lot of things could be "The P." But only one thing can be "The Big P."

I think he just gave me the introduction for my speech.

CHAPTER TWELVE

Beginning to Develop

One of my clearest memories of my own childhood is report card day, which occurred four times a year. Each student at St. Clare School would be sent home with a checkbook-green account of his or her progress. I remember my parents nodding their approval and then table-tenting my report card on the kitchen counter, where it would stay for at least a week, greeting anyone who might drop by through the back door and giving me no small amount of personal fulfillment. Before I was old enough to be graded on actual subjects, the assessment scale at St. Clare School had a very simple rating system: in each category, a student's work would be either Satisfactory or Unsatisfactory. Four times a year, I would take my report card down from the kitchen counter and gaze with great pride at my uniform rows of S's, a fleet of billowing sailing ships in Sister Angelique's best cursive.

Penmanship	*S*
Courteous Behavior	*S*
Uses Time Wisely	*S*

I would have accepted nothing less from myself, although if I were honest I would have admitted that getting all S's was not really that hard. I just did what was expected of me.

These days a mere report card is an insufficient review of any child's progress, and so David and I are obliged to visit the boys' school twice a year for a private conference with their teachers. It is there that our children's development (in kindergarten and pre-K, respectively) is reviewed in great detail: their playdeck behavior, their participation in music and Spanish and Show-and-Tell. We had already had about four of these meetings regarding Connor. Each one was mostly spent making small talk with his teachers. He was a birth order dream: the oldest child of two oldest children. Of course his report card had all laser-printed M's (as in "Most of the Time"). Really, there was nothing to discuss.

Now it was time for Seamus's pre-K evaluation, with the same teacher Connor had had the year before. David and I sat in two tiny chairs, our knees bumping up against the Choice Time table. Ms. Porter smiled, a little tightly it seemed, and placed Seamus's evaluation in front of us. I could see immediately that something was wrong. The letters were not in a uniform row. There were a few M's, but many more S's and B's:

Follows classroom rules	B
Responds appropriately to verbal requests	B
Uses words to express needs	S
Understands boundaries between self and others	B

I had to check the key to see that the "S" here meant not "Satisfactory" but "Sometimes"; in other words, *only* sometimes. The "B" in this equation was for "Beginning to

Develop," an optimistic euphemism, though I immediately understood its true connotation: Bad. Moving Backward.

"Seamus is having some trouble listening," Ms. Porter began gently. (A year earlier, she had told us what an unending pleasure Connor was to have in class.) "If we tell Seamus he has to listen, he will cry, and claim something is hurting him, but he still will not cooperate."

He cried when it was time for music class and refused to line up on his assigned number.

At recess, he had pushed a mild bespectacled boy off his tricycle and scratched a little girl, without apparent provocation.

In art class, he refused to participate at all, his Do-A-Dot landscape stubbornly blank despite his art teacher's encouragement. In the end, she had sixteen other kids she had to worry about, so for the last few weeks she had been letting him just sit there.

I was embarrassed by the tears in my eyes.

"I'm so sorry to spring this all on you," Ms. Porter said. "I would have said something sooner, but it's really all just come to a head. It must be something of a shock." But it wasn't. It was just that I had chosen to believe, while Seamus had become such a belligerent, weepy pain in the ass at home, that at least he was doing well at school. I told myself that he was coming home and detonating from the pressure of having behaved at school all day long. Children are always worst for their mother, aren't they?

That evening, David and I sat Seamus down and tried to discuss it. Seamus busied himself by chewing on his sleeve.

ME: Sweetheart, why don't you like art?

Seamus chewed for a minute, considering. Then:

SEAMUS: I do wike art.
DADDY: Do you like your art teacher?
SEAMUS: Yes, I wike her.
ME: Then why aren't you doing any work in art class?

Seamus shrugged.

SEAMUS: Sometimes I do.

He went back to chewing on his sleeve.

Ms. Tumulty, the head of the Lower School, requested a follow-up meeting with us to discuss Seamus's progress report. There was no such thing as a "Head of Lower School" in my day, but if there were, I can say with certainty my mother would never have had to visit her to discuss my behavior. Seamus was barely four, and here we were already being called before the High Court. "Seamus seems very unhappy," Ms. Tumulty said, businesslike but sympathetic. "We want to do what we can to help him succeed here."

"Maybe we let him repeat the year?" David suggested. "He *is* one of the youngest kids in his class."

Hold him back? I thought. *Let's not get crazy here.*

"When is his birthday again?" Ms. Tumulty asked, checking her notes. "Oh, right. Late July. Yes, you could go that way."

"When does the school make that call?" David asked.

Ms. Tumulty shrugged. "We don't," she said. "We leave that to the parents. Academically, I'm not sure he needs it.

Socially, he might benefit from some more time. There's lots to consider on both sides. The school will support your decision, but it is yours alone to make."

We couldn't decide anything right then, since David had to dash off to work from that meeting. Although I thought of little else all day, I waited until bedtime to bring it up.

ME: So what should we do?
DAVID: (setting alarm clock) About what?
ME: About holding Seamus back.
DAVID: Well, we're going to do it.
ME: What?
DAVID: Ms. Tumulty told us to.
ME: She said it was our decision to make!
DAVID: Yeah, but that's what she *meant*.

I had heard no such thing, but David had. Or maybe he just wanted to.

ME: She said there were lots of pros and cons to consider.
DAVID: I don't think there are any cons. Who cares if he does pre-K again? I feel fine about that.

Well, at least one of us did.

When it comes to life-altering decisions, true forks in the road, David shows breakneck resolution. Malcolm Gladwell himself could not make decisions any more quickly. David considers, makes up his mind, and sleeps soundly the same night. It's the little decisions, ironically, that throw him for a loop: "Would you like soup or salad to start?" can send my husband into catatonia. Once a week or so, getting dressed for work, he will pull out some conundrum of a sport coat, brown with orange windowpanes. "What tie?" he'll say, tossing three options on the bed.

I will glance at them for three seconds. "This one," I'll say.

"Really?" he'll answer, always, no matter which one I pick. "*Really*?" He'll hold it up, stand back, squint, choose another. "Not this one?"

This drives me nuts, because why did he ask me if he was just going to question whatever I said? Plus, in the case of blue checks versus red stripes, I am always sure I am right. But the ties don't matter, not in the way a life's path does, and I wish I could be as certain of the big issues as David is uncertain of the small ones. In this way, I suppose, we are at least exceedingly well matched.

Over the next several months, while David remained unwavering in his resolution to hold Seamus back, I changed my mind seven hundred times. There was no clear-cut answer. If we kept him with his class, and it turned out to be a bad idea, we would have missed the best window to make the change. On the other hand, if we "held him back"—and what parent could freely choose to do something sounding so horrible?— then we might be dooming him to tower, Baby Huey–like, over his classmates. (Thomas Trojanowski had a downy mustache by the time I was in fourth grade, and it irretrievably marked him, sitting among us at First Friday Mass, as the class dunce.) If we kept Seamus in his grade, his behavioral problems might continue. If he repeated the year, he could be bored and act up anyway. He might start cutting Morning Meeting on the rug to sneak outside and have a smoke.

The more I thought about either side, the more unacceptable it seemed. Keeping Seamus with his class became "pushing him forward," something I was unwilling to do. Giving him another year was "holding him back," and it was still hard to accept that a child of mine was not naturally at the front of the pack. What I wanted to do was allow him to stay where he was. No pushing, no pulling. But February 15th approached, and the school needed to know which of the two spots they were holding could be offered to a new student. (This was New York City, after all.) It was time to make the call.

When I am pressed to make a large decision about which I feel particularly indecisive, I get out pen and paper and create two columns: pro and con. I list all the reasons for and against my decision. Then I cross out all the ones that are hypothetical, leaving only the potential outcomes of which I am fairly certain. Usually, the answer is then clear, because one column will be much longer than the other. Despite my months of wavering, I will really have made the decision long ago, my brain waiting only for me to see the results in black and white.

This time, my paper had quadrants: Good Outcomes If We Hold Seamus Back. Bad Outcomes If We Move Seamus Forward. And so on. Boredom went in the upper right; Eternal Struggles went in the lower left. I regarded my four columns and could see immediately that the Good Outcomes If We Move Seamus Forward section was a little light on content. "Might turn out fine," I had written. Since that, by my own rules, was merely speculative, I had to cross it out, leaving that quadrant empty.

"I've decided," I told David that night. "Let's give Seamus another year."

"I'm glad you feel that way," David answered, half-asleep, "because there was never any doubt in my mind." I took comfort in David's fixed stance. It had to mean something. I hadn't said anything that changed his mind, whereas anything anyone said had changed mine.

Now there was only the matter of going public with it. I called the head of the Lower School. "I think you're making the right decision," Ms. Tumulty told me, and I wished she had just told us that in the first place. Then I practiced saying it out loud. "We're holding Seamus back," I started saying, unprompted, at Starbucks after drop-off. "It was totally our decision, but the school has been very supportive." I felt better having it known that it came from us. If there was going to be any gossip, I wanted to be clear: Seamus broke up with Kindergarten. Kindergarten did not break up with *him*.

Of course, as soon as we went public with our decision, Seamus had a complete personality transplant. He listened to his teachers, he participated with great attentiveness in art class, and he made a friend, a little boy named Austin who did a dance of welcome whenever Seamus entered the room. They hugged each other tightly each morning, reuniting joyfully after seventeen hours apart, tipping back and forth until they fell onto the floor in a pile of giggles. (This was acceptable behavior in Ms. Porter's pre-K.) It was like the shaggy hairstyle that starts bouncing and behaving as soon as the appointment at the salon is scheduled. I watched Seamus and Austin embrace, stricken anew. Had we chosen wrongly? If so, it was too late to change things now. Everyone had already been informed of our decision—everyone except Seamus himself.

David and I felt that there was no reason to tell Seamus until school was over, since it would probably only confuse him. Just five days after school ended, though, Seamus would begin the school's "June Camp," where the teachers would wear jeans, and hand out Popsicles, and perhaps not much else would be different—except that, when given the choice of keeping Seamus with his current class or putting him with the younger children, we had chosen the latter, so that he might make new friends before the fall. Seamus "graduated" on a Wednesday morning, all us parents snapping photos with our phones, the principal waxing on about how his group was "not in pre-K *anymore*," much to my chagrin. Seamus clutched his certificate with his off-center, shy smile. Camp began the following Monday. It was time to talk.

That Friday evening, I was getting ready to go out to dinner, applying eyeliner in the bathroom mirror while Seamus splashed in the tub. He seemed calm and content. I called down the hall to David, did an elaborate charade to indicate that the moment had come, and we began.

DADDY: Hey, buddy.

Seamus didn't answer. He was very busy with the bath toys.

ME: So, Shea, Mommy and Daddy have something important to tell you.
SEAMUS: (not looking up) What?
ME: Your school has changed a rule. If your birthday is at the end of July, or August, the new rule is, you go to Ms. Porter's pre-K, then Ms. Hanlon's pre-K, *then* kindergarten.

Seamus kept splashing.

ME: So that means, you're going to be in Ms. Hanlon's pre-K next year, instead of kindergarten.

Now he looked up at me. Getting it.

DADDY: And you know what else that means, Shea? It means you're going to be one of the leaders of the whole class! You will be the one who already knows what to do. You'll be one of the big kids.

He looked at Daddy. We held our breath.

ME: What do you think about that, Seamus?

He pondered. Finally:

SEAMUS: Did you know that Wightning McQueen has weawy bwue eyes?

He acted like he didn't care at all. I wasn't buying it. It seemed to me that Seamus, in a very male way, was choosing not to have the difficult conversation; it was not that there was nothing difficult to say. Surely he saw the hesitation in my eyes, as I saw it in his. But the decision had been made already, and had been made for him. Maybe he took some comfort there.

The following Monday I walked Seamus into his assigned room for camp: the nursery school classroom. He was the first to arrive. "Hello, Seamus!" his new teacher said, crouching down to his level. "I'm Ms. Warren. I have never met you, Seamus. Were you in the other nursery class this year?"

"He was in Ms. Porter's pre-K," I said, trying to indicate with my eyes that she should ix-nay on the ursery-nay. "And now he's going to be in Ms. Hanlon's pre-K!"

"Ohhhh," Ms. Warren said, getting it, but I could see her brain ticking: *What's the matter with this kid? How old is he? What have I heard in the break room?*

The next camper to arrive was a red-haired girl a full six inches shorter than Seamus was. The next camper, a little boy, showed up in a stroller. When I helped Seamus find his cubby, I saw that each camper had been supplied with a tub of Kandoo baby wipes. I waited for Seamus to announce, "Dis cwasswoom is for babies!" He did not. I waited for him to look around and say, "Where's Austin?" He did not. I waited for him to beg me, as he had almost every morning during the school year, not to leave.

Instead, he wandered over to a water table, little nets at the ready to catch plastic fish. "Are we fishing?" he asked the red-haired girl as an icebreaker. She moved over to make room for him.

"Have a great day, Shea," I said, kissing him on the cheek.

"Fanks," he said, fishing net in hand, and if he didn't seem overjoyed by his new environment, neither did he seem to mind.

That evening, Connor decided to make some polite conversation over their whole wheat penne.

CONNOR: Which camp group are you in, Shea? Are you in Blue?
SEAMUS: I not in bwue, I don't fink so.
CONNOR: Well, you have to be in Blue, 'cause all the pre-K kids are either Red or Blue, and you weren't with the Red group on the playdeck.

ME: Seamus is in Ms. Warren's class with some new friends! Right, Shea?

Connor's brow furrowed.

CONNOR: Mom. He can't be. That's the nursery kids.
ME: (rebranding valiantly) You mean, the up-and-coming pre-K kids!
CONNOR: (quite sure of himself) No, that can't be. That's so . . . *low*.

In retrospect, it had perhaps been an error not to alert Connor that Seamus had been redshirted. David and I had thought such information was far too dangerous in Connor's hands. "It's okay if you're not ready for kindergarten, Shea," Connor would murmur as they lay in their twin beds at night. "Don't feel bad. Someday you'll be one of the big kids, just like me." Information like that could yield years of knife-twisting. But now the cat was out of the bag. And Connor's bullshit detector was much more refined than his younger brother's.

CONNOR: I just don't understand why Seamus is with the nursery kids!
ME: He's not, Connor. All those kids are in pre-K now, just like him.
CONNOR: But, Mom. The nursery group is what it's *called*. That's its *name*.

Why this had to be the only camp in the world that didn't name their groups the Sharks and the Sea Otters, or the Shirts and the Skins, or whatever the hell, is way beyond me.

I have been waiting for Seamus to protest being in the nursery classroom as vociferously as Connor has on his behalf. I'm dreading the moment it dawns on Seamus that Austin has gone on to kindergarten without him. Maybe he understands that perfectly well already, but the way Seamus keeps everything inside, it's hard to tell. That's why this decision was so hard to make. It wasn't that Seamus couldn't grip his pencil, write his name, count to ten (in Mandarin Chinese). It was nothing that cut-and-dried. It was that we couldn't really tell whether he felt happy at school or not, and had no idea whether holding him back would make it any different.

Now, Ms. Warren tells me each day that "he seems fine," though it is clearly hard for her to say. When I ask Seamus at dinner who he played with that day, he says, "Nobody, weawy," but he seems perfectly content with that. Maybe another year in pre-K—the "gift of more time," as the head of the Lower School put it—will bring him out of his shell and make him the outspoken leader, handling his day with assurance and ease. But it might not. He might always hang back and keep things to himself. I might never have the gift of knowing for sure. The author Rita Mae Brown once said that a peacefulness follows any decision, even a wrong one. While this has been true for my own life, I fear it will not be true for the decisions I make for my children. If I'm waiting for a time I can stop worrying about Seamus and whether I have done right by him, it's not going to be any time soon.

Last weekend we went to my brother's wedding, a party my kids had eagerly awaited for months. Seamus wanted to wear his tie over his pajamas as soon as he woke up that morning. He looked impossibly grown-up when I dressed him in his navy suit. As soon as the band started playing at the reception, Seamus rushed the dance floor, kicking and spinning, completely carefree. This was not the timid little boy he usually was, the one I was expecting to see, and so I ran after him, yelled above the band, tried to take his hands and do some disco twirls with him, sharing in his delight. But Seamus did not want his hands held. He was happier without my interference. I went back to the table and watched him dance, too quickly during a slow song, too slowly during a fast one. It was a moment I was itching to fix, to render adorable; he looked kind of weird out there, flopping around all alone while everyone else was eating their salad course. But he also looked happier than I had seen him in months. Whirling all by himself, he was free of cares, free of expectations, free of the adult obligation to meet the beat in any way. He was free to be where he was, and just dance.

CHAPTER THIRTEEN

Penny the Pig

There are a few moments among the proudest in any mother's life: watching her baby take her first steps, for example, and then in a blink, watching that baby walk down the aisle to graduate or be wed. Perhaps the most bittersweet of mothering milestones occurred for me just this past spring, when Connor was chosen, out of all sixteen children in his kindergarten class, to be Person of the Week.

Every other child, to be honest, had already had a turn at this honor. The predetermined schedule had been sent home in September, and I had had the week of May 4th marked in my datebook for months, when Connor would become the very last child in his class to assume the mantle. Connor was awaiting his five-day reign with nearly breathless anticipation, and I could only hope it would live up to what were by then his rather elevated expectations for the experience.

In case you have not yet had this honor at your home, here is what each Person of the Week must provide:

- a collage of family photos for the classroom wall
- a painstakingly handwritten list of his or her favorite foods, books, and activities
- the filling of the classroom "Estimation Jar" with a secret number of delightful objects for the class to estimate and share the spoils thereof

All this was on top of the usual kindergarten homework: a list of words that started with the Letter of the Week (in this case, Z) and the procurement of a household object starting with said letter. It was a little unclear to me what the Estimation Jar had to do with being the Person of the Week, and why that responsibility might not be pawned off to a family that had, oh, a little less on their plate that particular weekend. But I did not complain. I was the mother of the bride, and the joy on my child's face when he was crowned Person of the Week would be reward enough for the busy weekend ahead.

The biggest payoff for being Person of the Week, as far as Connor was concerned, was that he got to bring the classroom mascot—an unassuming and sort of dingy stuffed animal named Penny the Pig—home for the weekend. "I got Penny in my backpack, Mom!" Connor yelled, in almost manic spirits, when I picked him up on Friday afternoon. "Great!" I said, grabbing the Estimation Jar, and we were on our way. When I hoisted Connor's backpack for the rainy walk home from the bus stop, I noticed that it seemed kind of heavy for only containing a stuffed animal, but that was just in passing. It was only when we got home, and Connor pulled Penny out of his backpack to introduce her to all our other stuffed animals, that I noticed there was an overstuffed binder crammed in there as well. "What's this?" I asked.

"Oh," Connor said, dumping out the hamper full of Penny's new friends. "That's Penny's scrapbook. We have to show the class everything she gets to do with us this weekend. Can we have a party?"

Here, laid out before me on the kitchen counter, was the chronicle of Penny's adventures with all the other families in Connor's class: an autumn camping trip; Christmas in Vermont; a beach vacation in St. Bart's; a figure-skating competition; a piano lesson; casual sushi making; and an elaborately choreographed jewelry heist, complete with sets and costumes, in which Penny was the sleuth who saved the day. Each family's entry was scrapbooked beyond anything I had ever imagined. One mother had used colorful adhesive photo corners to attach her family's photos and spelled out "MEMORIES" in mock-quilted sticker letters. Another mother had mimicked, in type style and story, the award-winning children's book *If You Give a Pig a Pancake*. I never made pancakes, ever.

Each entry topped all those that had come before. Now it was our turn. "So, who gets to see the scrapbook?" I asked Connor, trying to sound casual. (He was still party planning in the toy room.)

"Ms. Truman reads them to our class," he answered enthusiastically. "And ours is going to be the awesomest! Right, Mom?"

"Uh-huh," I answered back, suddenly understanding that my weekend was to be spent in frantic preparation for a project destined to be seen on Monday morning by an audience of exactly sixteen. Had Connor been the first Person of the Week, instead of the last, I might have assumed I could do something half-assed, a one-pager with two or three photos, and have Connor write the captions himself. I was relieved that we were going last so I could at least see clearly what was expected of me. I had to make up some lost ground with Ms. Truman, who I was sure already perceived me as a slacker mom. When the Letter of the Week had been J, and Connor decided to be five minutes late for the bus before he started looking for his household object, I grabbed a jar of Jif and shooed him out the door. At pickup that afternoon, Connor waited for me at the entrance to the classroom, holding the Jif carefully away from his body in a sealed Ziploc bag. "Mom. You *can't* bring peanut butter to *school,*" he hissed, cheeks aflame, and of course I brought peanut butter to school *every day* when I was in kindergarten, but today, you might as well bring in high-level radioactive waste.

On the other hand, there are times when I nearly kill myself with parenting effort only to find that I should not have bothered. When the boys' camp declared last summer that a particular Wednesday would be "Evil Superhero Day," I was up early laying out various costume options. Connor decided to be "Shark Man," and Seamus came up with "Bad Robin," the malevolent doppelgänger of Batman's ward. Off we went, me so proud of our family's creative accomplishments.

When we got to the parking lot, I noticed that none of the other campers walking in were in costume. A handful of counselors had made totally lame, five-minutes-previous attempts. "I'm Tinfoil Pinned to My Shirt Guy!" the head counselor said, waving to us from afar. "Hey, you guys look great!" But Connor was already pulling off his shark hat and rubbing furiously at the handlebar mustache I had drawn on him with brown eyeliner. Seamus's eyes were downcast in shame. I had gotten it wrong, again. Apparently Evil Superhero Day was only for losers. And their mothers.

How am I the only mother who always misreads these situations? Is there some clearing of the throat I'm not picking up on, some signal by which the other mothers can tell which assignments are to be ignored and which ones will count for 40 percent of our final grade? I can never tell if these things matter or not. Left to my own devices, I might have assumed that Penny's scrapbook was the *least* important component of Connor's rule as Person of the Week. I mean, it was unclear to me why the two were even related. But if the other mothers had put so much work into it, it had to matter. If I was about to overthink this, well, that was clearly my assignment.

Penny had been allocated to our family for what was fore-cast to be a very rainy spring weekend, one for which we had no particular plans. I was a little annoyed that Ms. Truman had handpicked for her own turn with Penny a long weekend on the slopes in Park City, so that *her* scrapbook pages might have adorable shots of Penny on the chair lift and sipping fire-side cocoa après-ski. After their busy weeks at school and soc-cer and karate, a weekend sitting around the house was just what my kids needed. But that was hardly scrapbook-worthy. Nor could I just make stuff up, since documentation was required. I couldn't say we went to MoMA without a ticket stub and a picture of Penny with a Matisse portrait to show for it. We had to come up with something good. And "we," of course, was me. Connor was already plopped on the couch, completely absorbed in an all-new episode of *Batman: The Brave and the Bold*, and David was not going to be any help either. None of Penny's scrapbook entries were in a father's handwriting. All of them had a clearly female touch, because the fathers had an ounce of sense in their heads. "Screw *that*," David would say when he got home, and I, while knowing his sentiments were correct, would still be the one a tearstained six-year-old would be pointing at on Monday morning if I didn't bother.

So there I was Friday night, doing a photo layout of our hastily arranged "Welcome Penny Pizza Party," in which Connor and Penny sipped an apple juice with two straws and fed each other pizza, like newlyweds sharing their first forkfuls of buttercream frosting. Next was bath time, requiring advanced trick photography to make it *look* like Penny was under the bubbles with Maggie without her actually getting wet. Then Seamus pretended to read Penny a bedtime story, me still snapping away. Getting my three kids ready for bed is usually activity enough; trying to make it all Penny-worthy was exhausting.

I tossed and turned in bed that night, dreaming of Penny, fretting about how to make her weekend with us one she would always remember. So far, we had not done anything that could be considered memorable. I did not want her going back to Kindergarten M and oinking about how lame we all were.

Saturday morning arrived with sheets of rain. My three children stared at *Handy Manny,* munching handfuls of peanut butter Puffins. "Hey, guys! I have an idea!" I yelled. "Guys! Let's create an indoor carnival for Penny!" The kids did not even look up. With forty-eight hours left to go, the novelty of Penny's visit had already worn off, and I was the only one whose oars were still in the water.

Nor was Penny an easy guest. It was exceedingly hard to tell whether she enjoyed making Shrinky Dinks or not. I started to think that Penny was a little bit full of herself: if Connor was Person of the Week, she considered herself Pig of the Decade. I was killing myself digging up arts 'n' crafts activities from the back of the closet and getting nothing but silence and an upturned snout in return. Meanwhile, it continued teeming outside.

"Who wants to go to the Children's Museum?" I hollered, trying to rally the troops.

"Not me," my children chorused, watching an old James Bond movie with Daddy on the couch. I couldn't get them out of the house. Truthfully, it was the kind of rain I would not normally have considered leaving the house in either. But we were not showing our guest a good time. The Flynns had taken Penny to Playland! We couldn't even make it to the mailbox.

By Sunday afternoon, I was out of ideas. It was still raining. Maggie was dragging Penny around by her curlicued tail and I did nothing to stop her. I wheeled Connor into joining me at the dining room table so we could at least start on Penny's scrapbook. We scrolled through all the pictures I had taken on the digital camera.

MOMMY: I thought we could show Penny asleep in your bed and say, "Connor's bed was so comfortable!"
CONNOR: Penny wouldn't say that.
MOMMY: Why not?
CONNOR: Because Penny is a pig. She likes to sleep in mud.

I hadn't thought of that. Maybe that was why she had such a puss on.

After several more such protestations that Penny would

never say that, or do the very thing I had created a photographic essay of her doing, I had Connor start on his "Things That Start with Z" list so I could just finish Penny's scrapbook myself:

> *Early Sunday morning, Maggie fed me some Raisin Bran. Yum!*
> *Then we got dressed.*
> *Then it was still raining so Connor's mommy said we could play the Wii.*

Oh my God. That was supposed to be the exciting part! Our scrapbook entry would go down in history as the worst weekend Penny had ever spent. Despite all my effort, here was documentary proof that all my kids did all weekend was lie around.

I had to jazz things up somehow, and so after the kids went to bed I downloaded scrapbooking software from the Internet. "You are nuts," David said, off to bed with a good book. Well, yes, but I was almost finished. All I had to do was teach myself how to use the software, then click and drag eight pages' worth of Penny's photos and caption them with zany fonts. Then, since there was no visible excitement in any of the pictures, I punched up my presentation with phrases like "Good Times!" and some clip art of a cartoon guy with a lampshade on his head. I was able to print out this magnum opus around 2:30 A.M., just in time to collate the family photos that I had suddenly remembered the Person of the Week also required, fill the Estimation Jar with Tootsie Rolls, and find a household object starting with Z. A tiny plastic zebra. Which I admit was kind of a cop-out but it was getting light outside.

Connor woke me up an hour later, anxious to begin the week at school in which he would be the star. I showed him the finished Penny scrapbook, our pages appended to the back of the volume. "What do you think?" I said eagerly.

"It's nice," Connor said, shrugging. A few minutes later, he used a tone that I perceived as slightly critical to inform me that I had not poured enough milk on his breakfast cereal, and that is when I lost it. "Can you give me a break? I was up all night working on that freaking scrapbook!" I screamed at my own son, the Person of the Week, no less. He looked at me, confused. Who had asked me to?

Back into Connor's backpack Penny and her scrapbook went for the trip to school. When we reached Kindergarten M, I laid out the Estimation Jar and all of Connor's family photos. Connor pulled Penny out of his backpack, tossed her on the LEGO table, and headed for his cubby. Forgetting something.

Mommy: Connor! Aren't you going to show Ms. Truman Penny's scrapbook?
Connor: Oh. Yeah.

He pulled the scrapbook out and handed it to Ms. Truman.

Ms. Truman: Oh. Yeah.

She placed it on her desk and walked away.

I wanted to scream. I wanted to throttle the carefree, childless Ms. Truman and say, "Do you understand what it is like to spend the weekend with a teething toddler crying on one hip while you give all your attention to a *stuffed animal*?" But I kept it together, still hoping that when I returned for pickup, Ms. Truman would lead all of Kindergarten M in a hearty round of applause: "Let's hear it for Connor's mommy, who has *really* outdone herself this time!"

She did not. Connor told me that evening that, since Morning Meeting on the rug had gone a few minutes over, Penny's scrapbook had to be scratched from the agenda. "Ms. Truman said maybe we'll look at it tomorrow," Connor added; I could tell he did not want to disappoint me. I did not ask about it again the next evening. I did not really want to know. It is possible that our adventures with Penny never saw the light of day at all, and that her scrapbook was trashed in early June, thrown out with all the ripply bulletin-board borders too covered in staple marks to be reused.

Once again, I had been had. Not only were my exertions unappreciated, they were not even noticed. However, had I handed in a picture of Connor's unopened backpack with a caption saying "This is where Penny spent the weekend at our house. Then she suffocated. The End," that would have been certain to come back and bite me on the ass. The things a mother does well are always invisible compared to the things she does badly.

The school year was over a few weeks later, but I did see Penny the Pig once more, sitting atop a plastic bin of stuff to go into storage. She returned my gaze impassively with her beady plastic eyes, offering neither gratitude nor farewell. Right up to the end, it was all about her. What a bitch.

CHAPTER FOURTEEN

Pretty

The Christmas that I was eight years old, Santa brought me what I wished for above all else: a My Friend Mandy. I was nearly too old for dolls, but Mandy was aimed at the more sophisticated consumer. Her pliant white Mary Janes went only on the correct feet, just like real shoes would. What baby doll could say that? Mandy's corn-silk hair stayed soft and shiny through all my ministrations, at least until I gave her feathered layers with my Ziggy scissors. Her eyes were blue, beneath impertinently long painted-on lashes; her smile was demure and complex; her body was a modest cotton unigarment, covered in rosebuds. I made a bed for Mandy out of a heavy-duty hatbox I decoupaged with strips of leftover wrapping paper. She lived in this bed, hidden beneath my own so my little brothers would not find her, amidst her alternate outfits: a pink party dress and white straw hat with coordinating pink ribbons; a gay red and green tartan frock for holiday wear. My Friend Mandy was not a rough-and-tumble backyard Barbie, one to share with the tomboy gymnast down the street. Playing with

Mandy meant, for the most part, sitting alone in my room, changing her outfits, and admiring her breathtaking beauty. The good people at Fisher-Price would have expected me to prefer the "My Friend Jenny" doll, since they had created her for girls who looked like me: brunette, freckled, green-eyed. But I wanted no part of Jenny. My Friend Mandy, with her blonde hair and rosy cheeks, was not only much prettier than I was; she was the prettiest girl I had ever seen.

Thirty years later, I am awakened each morning by a tiny voice calling me from down the hall, and each morning, when I go in my daughter's room to get her out of her crib, I am struck by how pretty she is. Maggie's little hands have five dimples each, where the fingers meet the back of the hand. Her cheeks are extra rosy in the morning. She also has lips that look painted on, pale blue almond-shaped eyes, and strawberry-blonde hair that lies straighter and shinier than My Friend Mandy's ever did. On most mornings, I bring Maggie back to our bed so she can give Daddy a wake-up kiss and get him in the shower. When David opens his eyes and looks at our daughter, he says, a little awed, "Sweetheart. Where did you *come* from?" Maggie doesn't look much like David or me. She is much better looking than either one of us. Perhaps, I sometimes think, she is a changeling.

I then take Maggie back to her room to change her sodden all-night diaper and choose what she will wear that day. The bowed, double-hung rods of Maggie's closet groan with the weight of her adorable outfits, both for the current season and the next three or four years hence. Imelda Marcos had fewer options. Maggie has so many enchanting things to wear that it is a little stressful trying to keep them all in rotation. I never thought that I would be this mom, risking debtor's prison to feed my Petit Bateau habit. I never thought that I would put more consideration than was healthy into what my little girl should be wearing to her "Free to Be Under Three" class on a Thursday morning, biting my lip as I considered whether her teacher there had seen Maggie in a particular frock before. But there I stand. "What about this one?" I say, pulling out a ruffly dress utterly unsuitable for a day Maggie will spend mostly hanging around the house. Maggie clasps her fat little hands together and inhales sharply. "Uh dess, uh *peh-ee,*" she breathes. She stays patient and still while I attire her in the dress, matching leggings, and her button-top ankle boots, giving her a sort of Parisian ragamuffin flair. "Yes, Maggie," I say, stepping back and taking in that day's masterpiece. "It *is* pretty." Then she makes her second grand appearance of the day before her father, who by then will be standing at the mirror shaving. David never fails to give the desired reaction: he hits the sides of his face with his open palms, in mock disbelief, and coos in falsetto, "So pretty! Who's so pretty?"

There is no question who has become, in David's heart, the fairest of them all. My heart always leaps a little at my husband's delight in our daughter; it has been a long time since he has reacted so enthusiastically to one of my ensembles. Of course, that may be because the attention that I pay to Maggie's beauty and wardrobe has come at the expense of my own. When I woke up this past Easter morning, I had no idea what I was going to wear to church, and from the depths of my closet, twenty minutes before Mass was due to begin, dredged up a blouse that (post-breastfeeding) gaped two sizes too large and a skirt that puckered about the hips in a manner most unbecoming. Oh, and I hadn't washed my hair. But Maggie's outfit—dress, crinoline, tights, and white patent leather shoes—had been laid out on her dresser for a week, chosen after great deliberation from several excellent finalists as I drifted off to sleep each night.

I am aware that I am on a slippery slope to Pageant Mom here. Not that I have ever dreamed of Maggie becoming Little Miss International Darling Grand Supreme. But now that I have a daughter, I get those women. Having others tell you your little girl has loveliness worthy of a four-foot trophy (and savings bond) is just as good as being lovely yourself, and maybe even better. When I walk down the street pushing Maggie's stroller, and Maggie walks beside me pushing her doll baby in *her* stroller, the construction workers no longer catcall at me like they did ten years ago. But every passerby gives Maggie a "She's so cute!" or at least the "awww" pushed-out lower lip, and I scoop these up as eagerly as Connor collects the blinking hearts he encounters playing *Star Wars* on the Wii. If I receive a compliment myself, I want to brush it off: "Really? I look like I lost weight? Uh, *hardly*." But hearing that my daughter is pretty is lovely and uncomplicated. I don't have to roll my eyes when someone says Maggie is beautiful. I just say, "Thank you," and I mean it.

I was not quite like this when my two boys were babies. I obsessed over their fat little baby feet just as much, and I heard they were cute when we strolled through the park too, but their adorability wasn't something I worked at. I mean, there wasn't that much to be excited about dressing them in. Only about 15 percent of the average baby clothing store is dedicated to outfits for baby boys. On that one, lower-level shelf, there is usually a serious overestimation of the average mother's penchant for camouflage, burnt umber and orange combos, and overalls so stiff you could correct scoliosis simply by wearing them regularly. I do remember one baby outfit of Connor's, sailboat overalls with knee socks and weensy saddle shoes, that was quite fetching. And once Seamus was born, I dressed both boys in coordinating mini-man ensembles for special occasions. But what they wear each day is not something I have tended to spend an excess of time, money, or brain cells upon.

Nor do I tell them, a hundred times a day, how handsome they are. I tell them what will please them: they're hard workers, they're good at coloring, they're super-fast. Their appearance only rarely enters into it—in their Halloween costumes, perhaps, or dressed in matching suits for my sister's wedding. (That merited a chorus of "You look so *handsome!*" from our relatives, which the boys accepted with good humor only because—like my lacquering of their cowlicks with my hairspray—it happens so rarely.) On an ordinary morning, when they stand at our front door dressed for school in their beloved Gap sweatshirts, I say, "You look so cool." To myself I think: *How cute. How handsome.* But I don't say it out loud. That would annoy them to no end. Their cuteness is not something my boys want pointed out to them.

But I do tell Maggie she is pretty. Many times a day. And she loves to hear it. Of course, she does not need to hear it, because Maggie is certain she looks gorgeous no matter what she is wearing: her brother's Yankees hat, her other brother's swim goggles, her beloved and pilly hand-me-down froggy pajamas. My daughter can truly make anything work. But when I tell her she is pretty, over and over, am I creating the desire in her to hear that even more? To prize beauty above all else? Doubtless I should be telling her other things: that she is intelligent and powerful, fierce and kind. All of which she is.

And once she is old enough to appreciate those things' worth, I fully intend to tell her so. But when she looks at herself in my closet's full-length mirror, resplendent in the wooden bead necklace Connor made me for Valentine's Day, I know what it is she wants me to say. And I cannot help myself.

I don't remember my mother telling me how pretty I was very often, although that may be because at a certain age, anything my mother said became an annoyance of the highest order. Just a few short years after my peak interest in My Friend Mandy, I asked my dad to take my picture for a modeling contest sponsored by *Young Miss* magazine. (Lacking a Pageant Mom of my own, I guess I took matters into my own hands.) Perched on our flowered sofa in the parlor, the "good room" where all our special occasion photos were taken, I am smiling tightly in this photo without showing teeth, bony in a teal velour long-sleeved polo, my permed hair a trapezoid, bangs hanging low enough to compromise my vision. I am the very model of seventh-grade gawkiness, even by 1980s standards, and I can't believe my mother let me walk around like that.

I was not chosen to be the new Young Miss of *Young Miss*. I was only a little disappointed. I did not really think I was as pretty as the real *Young Miss* teen models, who tossed their bouncy long hair as they skipped, laughing, down collegiate staircases in their plaid kilts with giant gold safety pins. I had sent in my picture because I wanted so desperately to be like them and understand what they had: something ineffable. Something I did not know how to get. They were pretty and they knew it. They were pretty *because* they knew it.

I wasn't bad. Okay, my perm was bad. But I thought my face, if one looked closely at it, was all right. It had potential.

I just didn't know how to be self-confident like the girls at Pia Perino's lunch table in the cafeteria. Those were the girls at St. Paul School who had their act together. Clearly, some of them had a lot to offer, like Melissa "Ton o' Tits" Tarowitz, who told me that Craig Harpin told her that he thought I was okay-looking except that I was flat as a two-by-four. I could not deny that this was the case. But it was also confusing, because Pia Perino was flat-chested too, and she was considered the prettiest girl in our class. Some of Pia's friends were neither particularly attractive nor well-endowed, actually, but they sat at her lunch table, and they were brazen enough to walk right up to boys and talk to them, and that made them, by group assent, the pretty ones.

I still think that being pretty is mostly about thinking you are. So how could it be a bad thing for me to tell Maggie how pretty she is every day? What if she could always see herself as I see her now: heartbreakingly beautiful, asleep or awake, in pajamas or pinafore? Would that not help her be at peace with herself through the rough patches ahead? Might those patches be a little smoother for it? All too soon Maggie will be in seventh grade herself, and heaven knows my opinion will no longer hold much sway with her. Certainly I will have lost the privilege of dressing her each morning. Already Maggie has begun tainting my daily wardrobe choices for her by insisting that every outfit be completed with her grimy hot-pink sneakers. I let her wear them because I want an independent-thinking daughter, and I am rational enough to see that no one but me cares that her sneakers don't match her dress. But I can also see that this is just the beginning, and that the ensembles Maggie chooses for herself may well become the source of our most fervent disagreements. Soon Maggie will get to decide how she looks, what image she projects to the world, whether to let the world see her as "pretty" or not. When that time comes, will anything I say help Maggie believe, deep down, that she really is beautiful, inside and out? Will she be able to see her reflection in her father's eyes, in mine?

When Maggie is grown, will I have been a worse mother for having told her she's pretty a hundred times a day, or having *stopped* telling her, so she won't think that is all girls have to offer? These days, we are told to praise our children, but not too much—that will make them unable to handle criticism. Buy them toys, but not too many; that will spoil them. Love them, but don't smother them. From all that, I can only conclude I should tell Maggie she's pretty, but not *too* often, lest she get the message that being attractive is her chief means of being of value. I shouldn't be the one to bring her looks into it. Maybe it's foolish to think I can make her awkward stage any less awkward. Maybe there is no seventh grader who looks in the mirror and *doesn't* think she is hopelessly unattractive. Even Pia Perino. It will be hard for me to stand back and watch Maggie be uncertain, even disappointed, in herself. But it also may be that an awkward stage is a useful part of growing up.

Maggie's favorite doll, at this writing, is not exactly as beautiful as My Friend Mandy was. "Baby" is bald, usually naked, not all that cute, and, since her left buttock indicates that she was mass-produced in China, Baby has probably been off-gassing toxic fumes around our house ever since Maggie received her last December from the Santa at the mall. But Maggie loves Baby, and to her, Baby is absolutely gorgeous. I sit on the old recliner in the toy room and fold a load of laundry, watching Maggie smother Baby with her nascent maternal instinct. "Baby need sock ons," she commands, and I dress Baby in a graying pair of Connor's I was about to fold together. Maggie swoons with delight. "Peh-ee Baby!" she says, nearly breathless. And I think, how can it be wrong to feel that way about your baby? And how can it be wrong to tell her so? I scoop Maggie up. "You're *my* pretty baby," I tell her, covering her chubby palm with kisses, savoring this reckless moment, heedless of loving her too well.

CHAPTER FIFTEEN

Mommy and Me

For the last four years or so—as long as my younger son has had the gift of speech—my two boys have assumed opposing viewpoints on everything imaginable. They are the most contentious siblings since the Miser Brothers (Heat and Snow). But just in the last few months, as my daughter has acquired her own gift of gab, Connor and Seamus have at last found common ground, something they can both enjoy ad infinitum: mentally torturing their little sister. Doubtless this will continue for many years to come; I have the sense they are just getting started. It's not like it's hard. Any time Seamus wants to get a rise out of Maggie at dinnertime, all he has to say is

SEAMUS: Maggie. Guess what. Mommy's weal name? Is not Mommy. It's Amy.

And Maggie, every single time, will go ape.

MAGGIE: No! Not—dat! No *not* "Amy"! No *my*! *Mommy!*

In her rage, she pounds her little fists on her high-chair tray. Her two older brothers fall about. I laugh too, in spite of myself, at her insistence (in the face of evidence to the contrary) that I belong exclusively to her. She will hear no talk of this "Amy," this alleged part of me that is someone besides her mother.

I suppose every one-year-old feels this way, but in Maggie's case, it's a little unexpected, because as the third child, Maggie has never really called the shots. While she has two older brothers to make her every waking moment a festival of lights, and while my mothering skills have probably improved and mellowed with experience, Maggie has never had me to herself. She and I never experienced the supremely dyadic, Chang and Eng life that my first baby and I knew: the world of Mommy and Me.

When Connor was very small, we were together—and alone—almost all the time. Being his mother was all I thought about, all I cared to do with my time. The days were ours, and before his second birthday, I took Connor to no less than eight different Mommy and Me classes. Each day these small-fry seminars take place by the hundreds, wherever the population concentration allows, offering babies instruction in everything from yoga to cooking, composition to theatrical dance. New York City boasts perhaps the world's greatest selection of Mommy and Me classes, and for this first-time parent, the thrilling array of choices was only somewhat marred by guilt that we were not taking advantage of each and every one.

No matter what education these classes claim to offer, no matter what dusty church basement they commandeer as classroom, they all have one thing in common: they are never called "Your Baby and You" classes, nor even "Mommy and

Baby," but always "Mommy and Me." This choice of names is not coincidental: it reflects the reordering of a mother's universe once her baby is born. The Mommy becomes a mere planet, a comet, even, a bit of dirty ice, hurtling around a newborn Me that exerts its enormous pull on her soul from the outside. Mommy is on Me's schedule, and since Me tends to dawn early, by 8:00 A.M. Mommy and her wee Me are both desperate to get out of the house. Mommy and Me classes offer, to the isolated new mother, both panacea and prescription: baby first, baby second, baby only.

If the name itself is not a sufficient lesson in proper maternal self-abnegation, further indoctrination awaits once class begins. Every Mommy and Me class, even "Li'l Tough Guy Sports Time with Mommy and Me," begins with a cheerful song of personalized welcome, going around the circle and acknowledging each little Me by name. "Hello, Heathcliff! It's good to see you! Hello, Abacus! It's good to see you too!" In this way, everyone learns all of the babies' names by week three, and the grown-ups' names, never. Why muddy one's head with such useless information? If the instructor needs to address one of the adults in the room, he or she can do it thusly:

INSTRUCTOR: Preston's mommy, would you mind opening that window right there a tiny bit?
PRESTON'S MOMMY: Um, sure.
INSTRUCTOR: Thanks, Preston's mommy!

Most of the time, though, the instructors act as if the grown-ups aren't even there. At "Broadway Babies: Mommy and Me," Connor's teacher would chirp, "Look at Connor doing such a good job clapping!"—tacitly ignoring that he was not old enough to sit up unassisted, let alone to rhythmically strike the palms of his hands together. But the rules of Mommy and Me dictated that we all pretend he could, and that I, as a mother, would stay behind the scenes, enabling the experience for my infant while not really being there myself at all.

Truthfully, I did not mind this. As a first-time mother, I enjoyed any construct furthering the notion that my baby really was the center of the universe, the most extraordinary patty-caker, splasher, and drooler that anyone had ever seen. Our Mommy and Me teachers were glad to support these delusions, and if they wanted to call me "Connor's mommy," that was fine with me: it was a hard-won title, and I was delighted to wear it, glad to have lost myself along the way. Without these classes, Connor and I would have had nowhere to go on a Tuesday morning. But a 10:00 A.M. "Run and Wiggle, Paint and Giggle (with Mommy and Me)" class at Kiddie Towne offered rough scaffolding for an entire day: getting ready to go, walking there, taking the class, maybe stopping for lunch with another mom and baby afterward, and doing an errand or two on the way home. By that time Connor would be thrilled to see his crib, and by the time he got up, it would only be three hours till Daddy got home.

There was only one fissure in this blissful, brainwashed time, one moment I sensed something was amiss. When Connor was about nine months old, he and I signed up for "Hands On! A Musical Experience! For Mommy and Me." The teacher of this class, a young woman with dreams of an operetta career, would have us rock our babies from side to side while she played the ukulele and prettily sang:

The more we get together,
Together, together,
The more we get together,
The happier we'll be!

That sounded good enough. But then she got to this part:

'Cause my friends are your friends!
And your friends are my friends!
The more we get together,
The happier we'll be!

I'd look around the circle, at the babies Connor knew well and the mothers and babysitters I didn't know at all, and think, *God, that is true. Connor's "friends" are my friends, and my "friends" are Connor's friends, and none of these "friends," the only grown-ups I ever encounter, have any idea who I am.* Suddenly, I was not so sure if, the more we got together at "Hands On! A Musical Experience," the happier I would be. But then the teacher would hand out maracas so we could "shake our sillies out," and Connor loved that part, and I'd forget all about being freaked out—at least until the next time I heard that song.

Our Mommy and Me pace slowed not a bit when Connor's little brother arrived, when Connor was a year and a half. Seamus napped in the stroller during Connor's "Afro-Cuban Percussion" class and on the gym mats during Connor's "Mommy and Me Big Muscle Workout." He had to fold himself into the busy schedule of his older brother, and he was, as second children are, exceedingly agreeable about it. It was Mommy who had a problem with it: by the time Seamus was six months old, my self-reproach that *he* had never been the "Me" in "Mommy and Me" became more than I could bear. I signed Seamus and me up for "Mommy Takes Me to the Water" class, also known as "Swimming," and immediately regretted this choice, since we both had to change out of our wet bathing suits in the locker room afterward, and there was nowhere to set my baby down while I changed, except upon the moist, fungal floor. By this time, I had also begun rolling my eyes at the twee hello songs, at the hovering, neurotic new parents. I just wanted the class over with; I had shit to do at home. But then I'd hear one of the other mothers mention some new class she and her baby were enjoying, like "Shake, Rattle, and Roll Over with Mommy and Me," and I'd feel ashamed. How could I have Seamus just in swimming? It was completely unfair to him! While I now had the suspicion there would be no lasting benefit to the two of us playing tambourine to a Laurie Berkner CD in the local temple's multipurpose room, I still felt bad that we were not doing it, that Seamus was getting, by any standard of measurement, less of me just for himself.

Two and a half years later, Maggie came along, and she didn't even get to go to swimming. Once the boys were in preschool every morning, Maggie and I would go right back home; any time I had "only" one kid in my care was a time to get stuff done. Mommy spent her mornings multitasking while Maggie/Me had rather excessive amounts of solo time lying on her Busy Bee play mat. After school pickup at 3:00 P.M., Maggie joined me as satellite around the elder suns, strapped to me in the sling as we made our daily orbit. If I had any remorse about this, it was that in a moment of third-trimester nesting extravagance, I had signed us up for an eight-week postnatal Mommy and Me yoga class. Five months later, Maggie and I had never gone. It was only the imminent expiration date of those eight classes, and $245 with it, that motivated me one February morning to put Maggie in the sling and jump on the crosstown bus.

When we arrived, I rolled out one of the blue yoga mats and lay Maggie down on it, next to my wallet and keys. Two other mothers showed up next. They chatted as they set up camp on either side of me: Marimekko quilts, multiple jangly toys, unscented baby wipes in on-the-go containers, graham crackers in Ziploc bags, monogrammed burp cloths. They lay their smiling babies amidst these small civilizations of attentive motherhood, then looked askance at Maggie, lying on the questionably hygienic yoga mat, chewing on my iPhone.

In lieu of a song, the yoga instructor had us begin by breathing with our babies, then introducing ourselves. "This is Desmond," the mother on my left said. "This is Samson," the mother on my right said. The mothers' names, as per usual, were not important (and who could top "Desmond" and "Samson"?). Quiet and respectful throughout our yoga practice, they restarted their conversation across my yoga mat as soon as we were finished:

DESMOND'S MOMMY: I'm so ready for it to be spring.
SAMSON'S MOMMY: I know. Everyone's sick. Did I tell you? I went to the doctor's office and the nurse goes to weigh Samson, and I'm like, did you Purell?
DESMOND'S MOMMY: Did she?
SAMSON'S MOMMY: Well, who knows? At least, she does it then. But then I'm thinking, she used the Purell, but she had to *touch* the Purell in order to use it. And who knows what germs are on the pump?

DESMOND'S MOMMY: In a doctor's office? Ugh.
SAMSON'S MOMMY: I was so grossed out I was like, don't touch my baby, I'll weigh him myself.

I was between them, rolling up the yoga mat, avoiding eye contact, pretty sure there was a hidden camera somewhere. Just then, another mother piped in.

ZAID'S MOMMY: You know what you could do?

I thought she was going to say "Refuse all medical attention." Or "Get a grip."

ZAID'S MOMMY: You could tell her to use the Purell like this.

Zaid's mommy demonstrated using her elbow to push down on the top of the pump.

DESMOND'S MOMMY: Oh my gosh, yes!
SAMSON'S MOMMY: I'm totally going to do that. Thanks.

At that point I was very glad I'd kept my mouth shut. After all, I'd brought Maggie there on the bus, and after I held on to the filthy communal pole, I wiped her runny nose on my mitten.

You cannot go home again. Mommy and Me classes are strictly the purview of the first-time parent, the mother for whom such exclusivity of focus is still possible. It would have done no good for me to attempt to inject some common sense into this conversation. These mommies would have taken one look at me and thought, *We're supposed to listen to you? You let your baby suck on your keys.* If I told them I was speaking from the experience of a mother of three, they would have been all the more horrified that my slack parenting skills had been visited upon so many. Even if I told them I once had a diaper bag well-stocked enough to compete with the best, who was I to try to introduce perspective into their lives, to rush the process of a first-time mom getting a clue? After all, no one had rushed mine.

Maggie and I did not return to postnatal yoga. Since then, for all three of my children, "Mommy and Me" time is a thing of shreds and patches. Mommy's taking you to the dentist to get two cavities filled! Just you and Mommy! Mommy is taking you to sit in the hallway during your brother's CCD class! Just you and Mommy! I sell these moments hard. My boys, knowing it's all they're likely to get, are not ungrateful for them. And after a typically chaotic afternoon of two school pickups and a playdate and karate and a doctor's appointment, I finally get home for good just in time for the babysitter to leave, her coat already on while she scrapes Maggie's dinner dishes. Maggie runs to me with mad abandon. "Mommy! Mommy home! You—you hold me?" she stammers. I pick her up, to give my baby thirty seconds of my undivided attention, and notice, with a start, that she looks different. She has perceptibly grown while my attention was not on her that afternoon, proof I have missed another day of her little life. When this happens I mostly feel sorry for myself; she is my last baby, and I know too well how quickly this all will go. But I feel sorry for Maggie too, and I wonder if it is wrong to sell her short. With two older brothers doing handsprings every time she learns a new word, she gets tons of attention. It's just that a lot of it is not from me. It's better for me that I no longer spend all my time in a "Mommy and Me" world. I'm not sure it's better for her.

I signed Maggie up for a "pre-nursery school" this fall. The only difference between it and a regular nursery school is that the grown-ups do not leave after drop-off, since the children are so young. Maggie loves it; every Tuesday morning, off she goes with the babysitter. "Mommy come too?" Maggie always asks, while Shelly buttons her coat. "Maybe next week," I say, and then, as soon as the front door closes, sit down to write in the rapturous two-hour silence.

But last week, I told Shelly to come in late. "I'll take Maggie to Mini Muffins for a change," I said. "It'll be fun." And it was. Maggie showed me her favorite pots and pans in the play kitchen and where she sat for snack time. I sang all the songs, I waved the multicolored scarves, and I was able to focus on my daughter, without distractions, for two hours. I enjoyed it. But it wasn't something I did every day.

As I buckled Maggie into her stroller, the instructor touched my elbow. "Thanks for coming, Maggie's mommy! I could see how happy she was you were here," she said.

"Me too," I answered.

"It's special. Right, Maggie? Wouldn't you like your mommy to come to Mini Muffins more often?"

"Mommy come too?" Maggie echoed.

"Yes, honey," I said. "I sure will. One of these days."

CHAPTER SIXTEEN

Disequilibrium

As a mother, one of the most taboo acts you can commit is admitting to having a favorite child. On the Bad Mommy continuum, it is somewhere just shy of abandoning your babe on a rocky hillside. I have never met a mother in real life who confessed to harboring a favorite among her brood, although in a recent study of British mothers, one in six of them (under cover of anonymity) admitted to having one. In all honesty, I cannot say I have a favorite child. But I have, at times, had a Least Favorite, a child who was driving me absofrackinglutely up the wall. The bright side to this is that my Least Favorite has changed easily and often, as my children share the claim to that title with one another.

People often talk about the ups and downs of a marital relationship and the tough-it-out periods all marriages must weather. There is good and inevitable bad whenever two people live under the same roof, but in all honesty, my marriage has been quite smooth compared to the patches I have gone through with each of my boys. They are, at this writing, only four and six years old, so I think that is more a reflection of how relatively calm my conjugal waters are than how rough the parenting-a-preschooler seas. Still, I have lived through tempestuous seasons with each of my boys, due to their phases of "acting out" (as misbehavior must today be called, as if the terrible twos are merely a sort of extended pantomime). Though I understood rationally that my difficult child of the moment was really crying for more of my attention, giving that to him was a challenge when everything *he* did seemed expressly meant to push me farther away.

But I have never heard the subject of the Child Who Makes You Want to Run Screaming from the House even mentioned in polite company, let alone a poll reflecting what percentage of parents have one. So I have always kept these feelings to myself, certain it was only my own children who baffled their mother with their ping-ponging between terrific and downright impossible. Then, in a used-book store one day, I found a parenting book from the early 1980s, the work of a child development study center called the Gesell Institute. This book asserted that most children alternate between stages of equilibrium and disequilibrium as they grow, every six months or so. When they are in a state of disequilibrium at, say, three-and-a-half, they will test the limits of their parents' patience on a daily basis. Six months later, at four, they will have matured into a state of equilibrium, and the problems of just a few months ago will be forgotten—until they mature another six months to four and a half years of age and return to their disequilibrial selves.

Here is the book's illustration of what this all looks like:

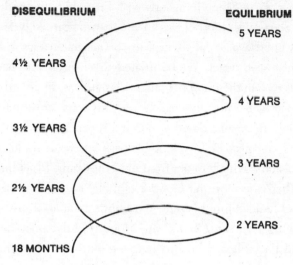

Figure 1

Alternation of Ages of Equilibrium and Disequilibrium

© 1976 by The Gesell Institute of Child Development, Frances L. Ilg, and Louise Bates Ames. Used by permission of Dell Publishing, a division of Random House, Inc.

This chart was so comforting I bought the book. For the first time, I had an inkling that my children's multiple personalities were not only not imaginary, but actually normal. My children, however, tend to make more immediate, Jekyll-and-Hyde switches between their bright and dark sides than the gradual, sproingy spirals reflected above.

When Seamus was a baby, David and I called him "Easy Shea," which is hard for me to believe sometimes, but I have it on video. While baby Connor cried incessantly, Seamus rarely shed a tear. He ate eagerly, took lengthy naps, and if someone wanted to hold him that was cool, but really he was just as happy to spend an uninterrupted hour with the pattern on his crib bumper, memorizing its whorls with his unblinking dark eyes. Easy Shea's older brother was an almost-two-year-old tyrant who threw unbelievable daily tantrums about scratchy tags in shirts, and plates on which ketchup dared touch peas, and bedtime stories read in the improper order. Connor was, I hesitate not to say, incorrigible, and although I knew this behavior was probably my fault (for having dared give him a usurping sibling), I more than once considered packing his bags for two-year-old reform school and leaving him out front until they came to get him.

Then one morning Connor climbed out of his crib, and when I handed him his morning sippy cup of juice, instead of throwing it, he said, "Sank you, Mommy." I did a double take, as did Easy Shea, who was hanging out on my hip gnawing on some zwieback toast. We both stared at Connor, the re-born angel, humming as he stood at his easel scribbling with broken crayons. The fiend that possessed him had been cast out overnight, and he was returned to me as the content and joyful little boy I once knew.

As soon as the rough patches are past, they are, like child-birth, the dimmest of memories. A year or so after Connor's transfiguration, I found a book I had bought during the dark times called *When Your Kids Push Your Buttons,* and while I could recall that I once had buttons that were repeatedly pushed by Connor, I could not remember where they were, or how. Per-haps I had matured as a mother, grown in patience. I breathed a sigh of relief: since I had evidently outgrown my buttons, I would not be needing this book for short-tempered mothers any longer.

And then, one morning last June, Easy Shea awoke as a kicking, screaming, recalcitrant, barely four-year-old stranger. His personal demonic possession manifested itself as a bound duty to disobey anything remotely resembling a direct order.

He brought multiple babysitters to the edge of tears. He would battle me to the death over putting on his pajamas or going to the bathroom, even when he had to go so badly his teeth chattered from the effort of holding it in. All communication with Seamus had to occur in a sort of logistical pig Latin, in that I had to twist around anything that I asked of him to seem like the exact opposite of my actual wishes:

> **Me:** Seamus! Mommy is going to be *really angry* if you open your mouth wide enough for me to brush your back teeth!

If he had an inkling it might please the person asking, he would not cooperate. Any attempts to discipline this child from the Bizarro world were futile, for he could always outwit with his line of opposite reasoning:

> **Me:** You are in time-out, mister!
> **Seamus:** I don't care. I fink time-outs are gweat. And I *don't* wike ice cweam. Or TV soes.

Seamus had found a whole new set of buttons on me that Connor had never considered pushing. The more I berated him, the more stubborn he became. He would get a time-out for sticking his fingers into baby Maggie's nostrils, serve his time, then head right back for another go at it. His behavior changed so absolutely and so quickly that David and I were sure something was wrong. He underwent a battery of blood tests at the pediatrician's. Nothing. We journaled his eating and sleeping and pooping habits. Seemed fine. We saw a psychiatrist, who was unimpressed by our Tales of the Hellion.

"He's acting out his negative feelings about his sister being born," the doctor explained.

"But that was eight months ago!" I answered. The good doctor informed me that there was no statute of limitations on sibling rivalry, particularly for a middle child as squeezed as Seamus was on both sides. "Give your son one-on-one, positive attention," the psychiatrist suggested, and I began picking Seamus up early from school so he could have me to himself while Maggie napped. At those times, he would be sort of weepy, but the psychiatrist was right—he would not act out! At least until the very millisecond one of his siblings reappeared.

This continued for an entire year, during which Maggie was the Amazing Smiling Baby and Connor was an absolute gem. There was a tacit understanding between Connor and me that I needed him to have his act together, and so he always did, with such aplomb that I sometimes forgot to mention it, even as I was heaping praise on his younger brother for not trying to stab baby Maggie with his fork for one entire dinnertime. Connor would tap me on the arm and say, "But what about me? Aren't I being good?"

"Well, of course *you* are good," I'd say, forgetting entirely that there was ever a time that was not the case.

I believe that mothering multiple children is only possible because they have this uncanny tag-team ability. While at all times one of your children is being impossible, it is usually not *more* than one at the same time. If the disequilibrium chart really held true, and children alternated between agreeable and challenging every six months or so, then Connor and Seamus, at eighteen months apart, would always be on opposite ends. There would also presumably be times when everyone met somewhere in the middle, and peace would reign for a while. But my children seem to stick either to the Very, Very Good or Horrid ends of the spectrum, as if on a carnival ride pinning them to either extreme by sheer dint of centrifugal force. Furthermore, they stay on one side or the other for what seems like much longer than six months. And so I believe that my children are all in on this together, holding whispered conferences in their pop-up play tent.

CONNOR: You know, Seamus, you've been unmanageable for a good while now. I'm glad to take it from here.

SEAMUS: Geez, that'd be gweat, 'cause I gotta tell you, I'm exhausted.

MAGGIE: I haven't even taken a turn yet, I'd be glad to—

CONNOR: No.

SEAMUS: Nah.

CONNOR: Seriously, it's okay, Maggie, I got it.

SEAMUS: Once you hit two and a half, Mags, you're going to be on duty for, wike, a year, so west up.

Call it paranoia if you will, but riddle me this: when I put Seamus to bed last Thursday night, it did not escape my notice that he climbed under the covers without any haranguing on my part. I paused at the door and said,

ME: Good night, sweetie.

and closed the door behind me. I could hear Seamus say something through the door, so I reopened it, steeled for one of his patented stalling tactics.

ME: What did you say?
SEAMUS: I said, "Good night, sweetie." You call me "sweetie" so I call you "sweetie." Night-night, sweetie!

That was weird. And then, the next morning:

ME: Get dressed, Connor.
CONNOR: But *why*?

Connor fell into no less than five sobbing rages that same day, over things like his brother bumping him with his arm as he fastened his seat belt, and my removing from the toy room a toy that he was not, at the time, playing with. We attended a friend's barbecue and made a memorable exit, dragging Connor to our car as he thrashed, sobbing, "Why do we have to go ahh no one else is leaving and I *will! not! leave!* Ahhh-hahhhh . . . ," and I was feeling, even more than embarrassed, completely freaked out, because Seamus was walking calmly to the car holding my hand, and not two weeks ago we had to get off a city bus and walk the rest of the way home because of the way *he* was carrying on, while Connor was being a saint.

Now it seems that Connor, at six and a half, has entered a phase of indeterminate length in which everything is going to make him whine in a manner so raising of my hackles I will have a hard time restraining myself from strangling him.

ME: What kind of bagel would you like, Connor? We don't have any raisin, but we have plain and sesame.
CONNOR: Why didn't you get me raisin?
ME: They didn't have any.

CONNOR: But I *really* wa-anteddd . . . rai-sinnnn . . .
ME: THEY DIDN'T HAVE ANY.
CONNOR: (breaking down) Why couldn't you—just
get me—a—raisinnn—baa-aa-gell . . . I wanted—
it—so—MUUUCHHH AHHHH . . .

This is the point where I bodily carry/drag him to any part of the house in which I cannot hear him, or at least will hear him only faintly, banging his fists on the wall and crying out to the gods that this "always happens to" him. I am not sure if ostracization is the correct disciplinary tactic here, but I am sure it is better than the Saying of Things Mommy Might Regret, or worse.

After a while, silence. Connor reemerges, sniffling, clearly attempting to function rationally. I, modeling coolheadedness, act as if nothing had happened.

ME: Hi, bud. Are you ready for breakfast now?
CONNOR: (lip quivering) I am. But, Mommy. Really. I
just have to ask you one thing.
ME: Don't do it.
CONNOR: Why didn't you—
ME: I'm warning you.
CONNOR: — buy me a—
ME: I'm begging you.
CONNOR: —raa-hay-hay-zinnnn BAAAAA-GELLLL . . .

And back to the whining corner he will go.

Is there any sound more grating to a mother's ears and more pleasant to a sibling's? Seamus looks on, savoring his sesame bagel, smiling fondly as he chews.

Seamus: I wike to wisten when Connor whines. I
twy to hear da words he's saying. But sometimes it
just sounds wike "Wahhhh . . ."

Maggie, looking up from her play kitchen in the next
room, also weighs in—

Maggie: Con-Con kyin'.

—and then returns to her morning creation, a frittata of
plastic strawberries and sporks.

Forty years ago, the child development specialist Jean
Piaget suggested that phases of disequilibrium in a child's life
are caused by their attempts to assimilate new abilities and
information. While a child is mastering a new ability, Piaget
argued, his brain is thrown into disarray. Once the skill is
acquired, equilibrium will return. I am wondering just what
new skill Connor is acquiring this summer that is making
his day-to-day existence so endlessly trying. Is it aiming Nerf
darts directly between his younger sister's eyes? Because he
gave that a whirl the other day and then argued tearfully that
I had never expressly forbidden it.

At moments such as these I hardly recognize my oldest
child, but I take solace in remembering it's not about me. He's
not giving me a hard time, the books tell me, he's *having* a
hard time. I can therefore meet Connor where he is right now
with a modicum of perspective, knowing that as soon as he
refinds balance, one of his siblings will leap to take his place.
If the good news is that only one of my children is in disequilibrium at a time, the bad news is that one of them is in dis-

equilibrium at all times. There have been moments in the last seven years when all three of my children have been sleeping well, not sick, and generally happy, but those times have come around about as often as a blue moon.

But while a mother's children get to take turns playing the heavy, the mother never gets to tag out, because all her children's disequilibrized antics, while aimed at a general audience, are really about getting a reaction out of one person: her. A mother's disequilibrium tornado is a thin one, always hewing close to the side of anarchy. And a mother's relationship with her current problem child will have a similarly narrow helix shape, veering from uneasy coexistence to times of prickly standoff, not once every six months, but once a day, once an hour.

No matter how often these standoffs occur, though, and no matter how skillfully her buttons are pushed, a good mother must not, under any circumstances, offer reaction or resistance. In its chemical definition, equilibrium occurs when a process and its reverse pull equally in opposite directions, so that no overall change takes place. But in order to neutralize a child's ranting, a mother is supposed to betray no sense of the surging tsunami that is within her, even after a two-hour drive in which she has heard "Mo-omm, he is *looking* at me!" no less than five hundred and seventy-three times. It is up to the mother, though she will live her life in a constant state of disequilibrium, to act at all times as if she is not—to be a paragon of moderate heart rates and vocal timbres. If she fails for a moment, if she meets a child's rage with a tantrum of her own, she will (so the experts say) have stooped to her child's level, and succeeded merely in creating *more* disequilibrium. I do believe that this is probably correct. I also believe that it is a hell of a lot to ask.

Maggie has not yet taken an extended turn as my most difficult child. Other than waking up an hour and a half earlier than I would like, she is a dream baby, and we are still in the throes of blind, utter intoxication with each other. "I Mommy's girl," she will say, snuggling her head in beneath my chin, and I think, *She will never betray me! She and I will exist eternally in this blissful codependency!*

I realize, of course, that it is folly to think this way. One day Maggie will ascend the Child Most Likely to Make Mommy Throw Something throne, precisely because she will be tired of having been so well behaved, and therefore benignly neglected by her mother, for so long. Headstrong as she is, I can also predict that her own periods of disequilibrium will likely put her brothers' to shame. But here is comfort: the laws of nature intend it to be this way. While disequilibrium may be the constant state of mind I have chosen for myself, it will only be like this for, oh, about another twenty years.

CHAPTER SEVENTEEN

Taco Night

One night last spring, we went to visit some friends who had recently moved to the suburbs. We were sad when Susan and Rob moved away, because our kids are all in love with one another, although it's very *Midsummer Night's Dream* because none of it is reciprocal. Their three-year-old is starry-eyed over Seamus, who in turn is gaga for their eight-year-old, who keeps asking us where Connor is. And so on.

Susan and Rob invited us over for "Taco Night," which I fully intend to steal as an entertaining idea if I ever start entertaining. I was amazed that Susan was managing to host guests just two weeks after moving into a new home. "Oh God, I just threw this together," Susan said in her new, enormous kitchen, where she had laid out little bowls of freshly chopped cilantro and minced jalapeños next to the taco shells and ground beef. There was plenty of wine, the kids would have fun, everyone would be fed from someone else's kitchen—this was going to be as good as a night off for me.

Susan and Rob's new house was gorgeous and a little intimidating. They had gone in a decidedly modern direction with the furnishings, and upon being invited into the living room David and I both stood there for a moment, not sure which of the aluminum-and-glass structures was a table and which a very low-slung and backless chair. "Where are the toys?" Seamus asked, always one to cut to the chase. (In our house, you can stand in the foyer and have seven Christmas mornings' worth of booty well within view.)

"They're in the playroom upstairs," Rob answered, firing up my real estate envy even further.

"Come on up!" the young hostesses called from the landing, and up the open-plan, railing-free staircase the two boys went, sixteen-month-old Maggie struggling to follow them in a half-crawl. "Want to join me in the kitchen?" Susan said. I looked at Maggie, wobbling uncertainly up the stairs. "Don't worry about Maggie. My girls will watch out for her," Susan added, reassuring me. I wavered. I did not want to be perceived as overprotective, but there was enough room between each step for Maggie to slip through and plummet to the high-gloss lacquered floor below. However, it seemed the Defcon Three alert was ringing in my ears only; Susan was already heading for the kitchen, and David was deep in meaningful conversation with our host. If the stairs were safe enough for Susan and Rob's two-year-old daughter to climb every day, maybe there was no reason for me to be such a party pooper. "I'll come out in a bit," I called after Susan, then sat at the bottom of the steps pretending to follow David and Rob's conversation while watching Maggie climb safely to the top.

A few minutes later, I excused myself to no one in particular and went upstairs to check on her and the other kids. The playroom was a lavender PBteen paradise, with a thousand stuffed animals and one large television deeply engrossing all the children in some Nick tween sitcom. Since they all seemed content enough—even Maggie, who was busily chewing on a stuffed rabbit—I returned to the adults downstairs. "Are they good?" David said.

"They're fine," I answered. He nodded and returned to his dialogue with Rob on the debatable merits of the three-point line in college basketball.

Okay, I needed to relax a little. The kids were all fine up there, at least until *iCarly* was over. I asked David to keep an ear out for Maggie, then grabbed my glass of wine and walked toward the kitchen to join Susan. I paused in the doorway; something told me to turn and look up. And that is when I saw Maggie, who did not know how to negotiate her way down *any* staircase, let alone one without a railing, stepping confidently out into space like a very young (and female) Mister Magoo. "Hi, Mommy," she crowed as she stepped into my arms 1.5 seconds later, having known all along I'd be there to catch her.

How did David react? He didn't notice. Engrossed in his PGA tour chat, he was completely oblivious to the death-defying acts happening directly over his head. As I carried Maggie safely to the ground floor, my heart hammering in my chest, I wondered: Why is it always the mom's job to save the kids from leaping to a certain leg fracture? Why is the mom the only one who even notices such things are *happening*?

Cocktails continued for another half hour before tacos were served. I had to save Maggie's life another eleven times. As David and Rob wandered outside to examine Rob's mulching efforts, David said, "I'll watch Maggie for a few." I quickly repaired to the kitchen, feeling guilty that Susan had been out there alone all that time. Two minutes later, I looked out the plate-glass window to see Maggie one centimeter from the swimming pool, behind my dear husband's turned back, while he was having a meaningful discussion about the continued relevance of the designated hitter in Major League baseball.

As I pounded on the glass, to no avail, then ran through the living room and out the front door to rescue Maggie, I wondered: Does David do this on purpose? So I will do all the child-chasing myself? So I won't *let* him take a turn? So I will always sit next to the baby (and/or crankiest child) on the plane, or at a restaurant, or in church? So that no matter where we are, the children are always, for the most part, my problem?

This is, in my house, how things have been divided: I am in charge of the children. For fifty dollars, my husband could not give you the name and address of our children's pediatrician. For double or nothing, he could not give you all three of their birthdays, plus our anniversary for another hundred. I know this because I have won all of these bets. David's brain synapses are not sagging with minutiae like our children's birth weights and current shoe sizes, or, say, what's for lunch. That's what I'm for. Where the kids are concerned, as long as I'm around, he can go off-duty in his head.

I think I am right about this. But if I bring it up, David will say, puffed up with hurt feeling, "Let me tell you something. Compared to some guys I know, I am not that bad." And really, he's not. If he gets home and the kids are still awake, no pipe and slippers for him; he grabs a kid or two and gets cracking, detouring to our bedroom only to take his tie off. However, he does have a suspicious ability to time his arrival for exactly *at* bedtime; Maggie will already have had her stories in the rocking chair, and the boys will be under the covers, leaving just enough time for Daddy to rev them all back up again. I can hardly blame him. Bedtime is my favorite time of the day, and why not just show up for that part if you have the choice?

But this division of parenting labor does tend to make weekends particularly hard. During the week, my kids have a clear routine: school, playground, dinner, bath. Once I got to three children, I also got a babysitter to help me with the staggered afternoon pickups and drop-offs and bath times, and we function quite well together. On a Saturday morning, David will grandly announce, "Let's all go to the diner!" and then disappear to the bathroom for half an hour with the weekend business section while I get the four other people in our household ready to go. Every once in a while, he'll yell through the bathroom door, "Let's go, guys!" as if (1) he is himself ready to go, which he is not, and (2) this, in itself, is making any contribution whatsoever to our departure. In the same time it takes for him to finish up, then brush his teeth and run a comb through his hair, I will have scouted the house for three pairs of sneakers, packed the diaper bag with a superabundance of crayons and juice boxes, changed Maggie's diaper twice, and dressed three unwilling children. Only then will David emerge from the bathroom, just in time for me to throw on a sweater from the pile on the floor over the sweatpants I slept in. Makeup? Why, I haven't even washed my face! Hair? Who has time for petty things like personal appearance? David is at the front door, natty as ever, yelling, "Let's go, guys!"

Weekends are exhausting. David does mean to be helpful—it's just that he never takes a turn noticing that it's already 5:40 P.M. and there's nothing in the refrigerator the kids will eat. The schedule lives in my head. When I ask my husband to help with an item on that schedule, he follows my request to the letter. Unfortunately, he will do exactly that and no more. This is probably an error of wording on my part. On a Sunday evening, instead of saying, "Can you give Maggie a bath?" I should say, "Can you give Maggie a bath, and then drain the tub, and take the towel that fell in, and find somewhere besides the bathroom floor for it to drip dry; and then take her to her room, and put a diaper on her, and choose a pair of pajamas, and then close the pajama drawer, and then put them on her, right-side out; and then comb her hair before it dries that way; and take her old diaper, and tape it shut, and throw it in the garbage can, rather than leave it splayed open on her changing table?" Of course, if I took the time to say all that, I could have just done it all myself. But if I am not that specific about my wishes, there is such a battlefield to be cleaned up in his wake, a swath of crap cutting across several rooms, that I regret having asked at all.

This may be calculated on his part. It certainly makes me feel like I am not free to leave all three children with him for any meaningful length of time. Once David offered me a "Mommy's Day Off" for my birthday, a quiet summer Saturday when Seamus was barely a year old and Connor was two and a half. I had known this day was coming for a week, which was good, since it took me that long to prepare the snacks, and the meals, and the outfits, and the backup outfits, and the proposed itineraries for their day. I was up early for my day off, out of the house by 8:30 A.M., cell phone left behind. I was off the grid and dizzy with the thrill.

I took myself to breakfast, my foot tapping impatiently for the check. I went shopping and didn't buy anything. I sat at the park and read without comprehending. By 3:00 P.M. I was out of ideas, and returned home ahead of schedule to find both boys still in their pajamas, Seamus with his diaper on *from the night before*. Connor was drinking from a sippy cup I had last seen six months earlier, before it rolled under the couch. The house looked like it belonged to one of those compulsive hoarders you see on A&E, narrow walking paths laid out through piles and piles of Duplo blocks and torn bits of paper. "We watched a *lot* of shows!" Connor yelled by way of greeting. And I spent the rest of my birthday working twice as hard to catch up as if I had never left the house in the first place.

What really chapped my fanny was that David seemed to think he'd been me for the day, and golly, that wasn't hard at all! If he "babysits" (his word) and the kids aren't locked out or missing limbs when I get back, he expects a ticker-tape parade's worth of gratitude. "Aren't you even going to thank me for unloading the dishwasher?" he asked me one night as I lay beached on the couch watching television for twenty minutes before bed. I snapped back, "Yes, I am. *Thank* you. Now, are you going to thank me every single other night, when *I* unload the dishwasher?"

I'm used to our division of labor at this point. I just want my husband to *get* that he doesn't do a whole hell of a lot—or at least that what he considers "a lot" is not the half of it. And that is where our opinions differ. We bicker about it every couple of months, and sooner or later, David always plays the same trump card: "I'm *way* more helpful than our dads were." Argument ender. He has a point.

My parents came to visit us right after Seamus came home from the hospital. David's best friend Jon had sent over his trademark lasagna (by the way, Jon and his cooking skills are always *my* trump card in the aforementioned disagreement). I had set the lasagna on the kitchen counter so everyone could heat up his or her own dinner when the mood struck. "What's for dinner?" my father asked me as I struggled to latch Seamus on to my enormous, postpartum bosom.

"It's *in the kitchen*," I answered through gritted teeth.

He walked out to the kitchen, where he stared at the lasagna pan for a moment, then called out to my mother, "Nancy, I'm ready for my dinner now." He had no idea how to render the cold, plastic-wrapped lasagna suitable for consumption; after all, his dinner had always been served to him hot.

Then there's my sweet and gentle father-in-law, who asserted shortly after Maggie was born that fathers did not change their daughters' poopy diapers, as if this were a matter of common knowledge. When I pressed the issue, he explained that he had himself never changed his two daughters' diapers, because as a male, he was ill-equipped to negotiate all their "nooks and crannies." David laughed so hard his Coke Zero came out his nose. His father took his lumps with good grace, but both he and my mother-in-law seemed genuinely surprised that David and I might do things another way.

There, I think, is the rub: the difference between our generation of parents and the one that raised us is that back then, our fathers were never really expected to help in the first place. If you needed help, your mother lived next door;

at least that's how it happened in Scranton. Now, we mothers expect our husbands to participate, and ever since he was in the delivery room to cut our children's umbilical cords, David has been more hands-on than his father ever dreamed of being. But I cannot say that our day-to-day division of household labor is that different from the way our parents did things. David goes to work every day, and I am (more or less) at home. We both agreed that it should be this way. As an actress, I was unemployed about 80 percent of the time, so I could hardly stake claim to being our primary breadwinner. Plus, as the oldest of six, I had vast child-care experience and maternal inclination to boot. It was the right choice for us. But sometimes I want to be the guest star. I want to be the one who swoops in five minutes before bedtime, Greco-Roman-wrestles the boys into a frenzy, and then gets on a conference call. I want to let someone else pack the diaper bag, or keep Maggie from falling in the pool, for a change.

Barring that, I want my husband to at least give me credit for how much I am juggling. I have never thought David is some benighted chauvinist. But on a sunny Sunday afternoon, when I have all three kids at the supermarket and David is gone golfing for eight hours, it is hard not to harbor some resentment while standing in the checkout line. One day there was an Orthodox Jewish mother in front of me in line, balancing her groceries atop her double stroller with three kids inside. I imagined what her household must be like. Built on the ancient bedrock of Tradition, I assumed. God, her husband probably never lifted a finger. Wasn't she tired of it all? But if she had any simmering anger, I could not see it.

When I saw a flyer a few days later advertising a seminar called "Manage Your Mothering Time" at the local Chabad

Center, I knew I had to go, if only to pick up a few pointers on how to get it all done without choking on one's own resentment. Though the flyer had stipulated that all were welcome, I wondered too late, as we went around the room introducing ourselves, whether that included a mother of children named Connor and Seamus, a mother dressed in jeans and a T-shirt. But none of the dozen or so Orthodox mothers gathered seemed to mind.

The moderator of the discussion, a woman named Esther, had her baby with her—her ninth, she told us. She dandled him tummy-down across her knee in a vaguely distracted way for our entire conversation. I don't think she looked down at him once. Nor did he make a peep. Esther knew her stuff.

Esther began by discussing the importance of organization for any mother. "I find I do best," she said, "when I know who our guests for Friday's Sabbath dinner are by no later than Monday evening." All the other women nodded, dutifully transcribing this in their notebooks and PDAs. "Then you marinate your brisket or whatever on Wednesday," Esther continued, "and start your challah on Thursday, so the yeast has time to rise overnight." I sat there thinking of my wedding china, still sitting in its protective Styrofoam wrapping. I had never had anyone over for a formal dinner, ever. Even Taco Night was beyond me. These women used the good crystal *every Friday*? I no longer felt like I could claim to be overwhelmed. A typical Friday night, for me, was ordering in Thai food when David got home from the gym.

When it was time for questions, I was gratified to hear at least some expression of bitterness from one of the mothers present. "If I ask my husband to watch the baby while I make dinner," she said, "he'll do it for a few minutes, but then she's back out in the kitchen, clinging to my legs while my husband reads the newspaper." *Right on, sister,* I thought to myself. *Awaken the feminist within!*

"This is something we all struggle with," Esther said sympathetically. "Men do not help like they should." The other mothers nodded.

"The Talmud has a saying about this," Esther said, continuing as we all leaned forward in our chairs. "*Nashim datan kalot.* Now, this has traditionally been translated as 'Women's knowledge is light,' meaning that our minds are simple. Fit only for household matters."

Aha! I thought as I scribbled. *This bullshit goes way back.*

"But the more accurate translation," Esther said, "is 'Women's knowledge is light footed.' We can do many things lightly. Men cannot do more than one thing at a time. We women can. *Baruch Hashem.*"

Nashim datan kalot, I wrote in my notebook, hoping I was spelling it more or less correctly. Esther was not saying her mind was more lightweight than her husband's. She was saying that, unlike him, she could multitask like you read about. I imagined Esther on a Friday afternoon, preparing for her dinner guests, her own Taco Night. As she pulled the challah out of the oven with one hand, she would get out the Shabbat candles with the other, all the while keeping the baby's bouncy chair going with her foot. The plumber would have shown up to fix the toilet in time for sundown, the phone would be ringing, and three of her other kids would be throwing all the couch pillows on the floor, jumping on them, and yelling loud enough to be heard down the street. Amidst all of this, Esther would look down the hall into the living room to see her husband, relaxing on the couch with an early-arriving dinner guest, discussing the Torah. Or Duke's coaching strategies for the upcoming NCAA season. Esther would look at her husband, sitting there doing nothing, and think, *Bless him. Bless his feeble mind.*

CHAPTER EIGHTEEN

Inhumane

"We're doing it tonight," David said.

How I dreaded those words.

I should have been feeling invincible. I had, after all, just faced down the unholiest of childhood ailments, the tenacious and onomatopoeically named Coxsackie disease. (I hesitate to even invoke its name in print; perhaps you should go outside and turn around three times after reading this paragraph.) There are many greater dangers to a child's health than the Coxsackie virus, but only Coxsackie, with its rash of tiny blisters in the mouth and back of the throat, will make your child so cranky and clingy you will long for some good old appendicitis.

Maggie, at one and a half, was at the tail end of her Coxsackie experience. After a weekend of a low fever, no sleep, and so much crying I never put her down, I called her pediatrician, who phone-diagnosed it as garden-variety teething. Once it went on for two more days, it was the nurse practitioner who discovered the abscesses in Maggie's throat.

As Maggie sniffled in my arms, recovering from the indignity of the tongue depressor, I asked the nurse what course of treatment she recommended. "Motrin and time," she said, shrugging sympathetically.

I had already given Maggie plenty of each, but it didn't seem to help much, especially at night, when she had nothing to distract her from the pain. I had spent the better part of a week rocking her to sleep only to have her wake up as soon as I tried to lay her down in her crib. In an act of desperation late one night, I brought her back into bed with me. I was sure it wouldn't work. None of our kids ever slept in our bed with us; no matter the hour, if they were in Mommy and Daddy's bed, it was playtime of the most exciting sort. This time, though, Maggie was so exhausted that she fell asleep on my chest almost instantly, her feverish head radiating heat across my chest that was not at all unpleasant. David had willingly decamped to the couch, and for the next four nights, Maggie slept in our bed with me, happily and relatively soundly. If she whimpered, I was able to soothe her back to sleep before either one of us really woke up.

But payback time had come, as it must. "She's better, Ame," David said, putting on his cuff links one morning as he stood over Maggie and me, still under the covers. "We don't want to get in a bad habit. Starting tonight, we have to let her cry it out."

Out of all the unpleasant duties one has as a parent, "crying it out" is the one I have gone to the greatest lengths to avoid. From the beginning, I have tried to ingrain each of my babies with excellent sleep habits (not counting Connor's reflux days). I would put my babies down in their cribs, swaddled within an inch of their lives, sleepy but, for heaven's sake, not yet asleep. They fell asleep alone, and on their own, and I confess to committing the deadly sin of pride whenever someone expressed astonishment that it took sixty seconds for me to put all three of my children to bed.

With each of my children, though, there have been times of 3:00 A.M. tough love, necessitated by illness or visiting relatives or incoming molars. According to the laws of "crying it out," the only way to train (or retrain) a child to fall asleep on his own is to leave that child in his crib, to heave and bellow and rend his garments. You may visit at increasing intervals, to assure your child that he is safe, but under no circumstances do you take him out of his crib. Eventually, he will cry himself to sleep. After an unpleasant night or two, your child will sleep through without waking, and so will you.

There are many who say this is unthinkable child warping. Your baby cries out for you, and you *ignore* her? How will she ever feel secure in this world again? I saw the merits of this argument, and also knew from experience that "crying it out" usually refers to the traumatized mother's reaction at least as much as the infant's. I dreaded the coming evening's events more than the contagion of Coxsackie itself. I would gladly have taken my own set of throat blisters over what was about to come.

Night One

I put Maggie in my bed at her bedtime and, when 10:00 P.M. comes, transfer her to her crib. She cries out for a moment, then rolls over and goes back to sleep. *My God,* I think, *this is going to be fine,* and go back out to the den to celebrate with two more hours of worthless television.

I go to bed at midnight. At one thirty, I hear the wail of what my dream at first tells me is a faraway but insistent ambulance. "Moh-AAHHH-oh-MEEEE . . . Moh-AAHHH-oh-MEEEE . . ." I sit up, like a bride of Dracula, and prepare to stagger to my master. "Leave her," David says in the dark.

I listen for ten minutes exactly, judging by the bright blue alarm clock on David's side of the bed. Then I go into her room to try to soothe her back to sleep. Maggie reaches her chubby arms up to me, and when I say, "Sweetie, it's time for night-night," she utterly loses her shit.

I beat a hasty retreat. Now I am supposed to let at least twenty minutes go by before I return. After seventeen minutes of unabated howling:

ME: What if she wakes the boys?
DAVID: She won't.
ME: Oh come on, they're going to sleep through this?
DAVID: They have so far.

We lie there listening. Once the clock says twenty minutes have elapsed, Maggie sounds like a car alarm that has been going off for three days, about to finally drain its battery: "UhhhwaaaAHHHoooo . . . WAAhhhoooommm . . . omm . . . eeee . . ." According to the rules of crying it out, this is a crucial game-changer. If the baby sounds like she's giving up, you do *not* go in, even if the clock indicates you may, because you may already have won.

Maggie is quiet for five full minutes. I close my eyes and instantaneously enter a REM cycle. Then Maggie starts hollering again, with renewed energy.

ME: What if she's still sick, and we're letting her cry?
That's inhumane.
DAVID: Yes, that would be. Inhumane.

Maggie is keening, a lamentation of her own invention. It is killing me.

ME: But if she's *not* sick, and I go get her now, then I let her cry for half an hour for nothing.
DAVID: That's also true.

We are quiet for a moment.

ME: Thirty-five minutes, actually.

I turn the alarm clock away from me. It is not helping. The digital readout shines a blue nimbus on the wall.

ME: Why would she cry like this if she's *not* sick?
DAVID: Because she wants to be in here with us?
ME: Yeah, but is it worth crying thirty-eight minutes over?
DAVID: I don't know.

I find this maddening. He refuses to take a stand, so that whatever I do, should it turn out to be the wrong thing, he can say he advocated the opposite.

ME: You always do this.
DAVID: No I don't.
ME: If you really agree with me that we *might* be

being inhumane, how can you just lie there?
DAVID: Go ahead. Get her.

I get out of bed, relieved he's giving me permission.

DAVID: But if you bring her in here, and she goes
right back to sleep, then you'll *know* she's not sick.

Way to play both sides, Dr. Sears.

Maggie does go back to sleep between us after only a
modicum of fuss but, with dawn's first light, is sitting up
between us, crowing, "Hi Mommy! Hi Daddy! Mommy-
daddy wake up!" as if it is high noon rather than 5:00 A.M.
She shows no memory of the night before. I feel like Wile E.
Coyote when the Road Runner shouts "Meep meep!" and the
coyote understands that he has, once again, been had. How
can she have slept only six hours last night, including a two-
hour break in the middle, and be *smiling* this morning? What
the hell is there to smile about?

Night Five

Clearly Maggie is no longer sick, but after beating me into
co-sleeping submission for the better part of a week, she is
drunk with power. "Mommy bed!" she bellows at bedtime,
pointing down the hall. I deposit her in her crib, where she
stands roaring, rattling the bars as if in Attica. David and
I are already fifteen minutes late for a dinner reservation;
the rookie college-aged babysitter stands in the hallway,
ashen-faced. In desperation, I lose my slingbacks and climb

into the crib with Maggie, who lays her sweaty head down and falls into dreamless slumber in about forty-five seconds. After ten minutes of slow-motion contortions to pole-vault myself over the side of the crib, I am free, and Maggie is still asleep. At the moment I consider this a big step forward. When she wakes at 11:00 P.M., 1:00 A.M., and 4:15 A.M., demanding I climb back in the crib with her each time, it seems less so.

Night Eight

Honestly, who is in charge here? Tonight she will remain alone in her crib from 7:00 P.M. to 6:00 A.M., a reasonable expectation for a young lady of her age. No matter what, I am *not* taking her out.

After ninety minutes of crying, beginning at 2:30 A.M.:

Me: If I bring her back into bed with us right now, maybe she'll sleep until seven.

David's breathing is heavy. He does not answer.

Me: If you were me, what would you do right now?

David just lies there.

Me: I want you to just *tell* me what to do. Basically. Is what I'm saying.
David: Well. I'm not sure.
Me: *Thank* you.

Maggie yowls away.

ME: So what should I do?

David snores.

It always amazes me that David can fall back to sleep at such a moment. His own flesh and blood is screaming like she is being stuck with a series of rusty pins, and David can doze off to it, as if he were being lulled by lazy waves lapping the shore outside his five-star villa. I think this says less about him than it does about me. Maggie's cries are physiologically designed to turn me inside out. The perpetuation of the human race must have depended on it *really* bothering the cavewoman when her baby cried, so she'd figure the whole breastfeeding thing out. We modern mothers are hardwired with this vestigial remnant of our former selves. Let's face it, Maggie's not calling Daddy a hundred thousand times a night, probably because she knows it would be a waste of her time.

How I wish I could go back to sleep like that. When I was pregnant I had terrible insomnia and was often up for a few hours in the middle of the night. That insomnia was kind of fun; I watched bad TV and ate Bellybars and did my taxes, all in the wee small hours, all alone. This is nothing like that. I lie there in the dark, listening to her wail, working a tessellation of if/thens without solutions. Let her cry? Bad mother. Go in to her? Bad mother. I lie there paralyzed, incapable of any action except that of hating my own life.

Night Thirteen

I have made considerable progress: I no longer actually have to be *in* the crib with Maggie, so long as I stand there, rubbing her back in counterclockwise circles, until she falls completely asleep. Since her internal sensors will then detect the slightest motion, even with her eyes closed, I drop to the floor, crawling out of the room with painstaking slowness. I make it to the door, closing it behind me with the quietest click I can manage. She is immediately, and fully, awake. Lather, rinse, repeat. After the first few rounds, I start leaning over the slats of the crib and getting a few minutes of shut-eye there myself, like a soon-to-be-disqualified danceathoner.

Night Sixteen

We are away with the kids for a long weekend. I have placed Maggie in a Pack 'n Play in the downstairs guest bedroom, hoping that her crying might not reverberate quite so loudly from there. But when she whimpers at 4:30 A.M., I hear her immediately and stumble to the bedroom door without even waking up fully. At the door, something stops me. *Honestly, screw this,* I think, closing the door. *She can wait until 5:00.*

At 6:45, Connor opens our door. "Maggie's crying down there, Mom," he says nonchalantly. I run down the stairs, overcome with remorse for the tearstained, sobbing sight that surely awaits me. Instead, Maggie waves to me from the Pack 'n Play, crowing, "Hi, Mommy!" The Road Runner was still saying "meep meep!" but Wile E. had won the round. Maybe Maggie had gone back to sleep, and maybe she cried for two hours, it was hard to say; but since she wasn't scarred for life by it, mine was not to reason why.

Night Twenty

Home from our little vacation, David and I are sure we have won. We have slept past 6:00 A.M. for the last three nights; so, we assume, has she.

At 4:00 A.M., Maggie starts crying out: "Mooommmm-mmyyyy . . . Wheh ah yoooo, Moommmmmyyy . . ." Sixty minutes later, she has hollered this another three hundred and forty-two times. I barrel down the hall to her room. "Now you listen to me, young lady! You go *back to sleep right now!*" Maggie screams, squeezing huge, hot tears of rage down her cheeks. We have gotten nowhere. I prayed for a strong-willed daughter, and I have received one.

At five thirty, David brings her back to our bed before he staggers to the shower. "I'm mad at you, Maggie," I say. "Look at Mommy's mad face." She regards me seriously but without fear. *I own you,* is what she's thinking.

"I can't do this," I say to David when he reemerges from the bathroom. "I can't get up at four o'clock in the morning every day."

"I know," he replies. "But it's not really your fault."

Hmm?

"Not *really* my fault?" I sputter. "Seems to me it's not my fault *at all.*"

"Well, no, I just meant—"

"Seems to me that the only blameless person *here* is me," I continue. "If you disagree with how I'm handling things, perhaps you'd like a turn."

"I say we stick her in a Pack 'n Play in the kitchen tonight," he says.

"Maybe *you* should go sleep in a Pack 'n Play in the kitchen tonight," I say.

I have crossed over to enemy territory. I have Stockholm syndrome. I kind of *liked* having her in the bed with me all night. At least we were all sleeping then. Looking through the gauze of my lobotomized, sleep-deprived brain, it's hard to remember why I'm attempting to change things at all.

But David is right: enough is enough. We need to change back to the way things were. Because he is tired of the couch. Because we were all sleeping better six months ago. Because I am in charge, goddamnit, and it's time I impressed that upon her somehow. Because, although she is cuddled up against me now in a fetal comma, Maggie is closer to two than to one. She is not a baby anymore.

I know that something will work eventually. Both of Maggie's brothers went through stages when they woke up far too early, but I only remember that now because I wrote it in the baby calendars I dutifully kept on their changing tables. I don't recall how it happened, but they don't wake up at 4:00 A.M. *now*, so it ended at some point. If only Motrin and time cure the horrible Coxsackie, perhaps only coffee and time will cure this mother and her wakeful baby. Until then, letting her cry may be inhumane—against every fiber of my maternal being—but I humbly submit that in our inhumanity contest, the one being most cruel and barbaric, callous and ruthless, is the one of us weighing less than twenty-five pounds.

CHAPTER NINETEEN

Liar, Liar

I have always found it comforting that while my children each have numerous challenging qualities, lying is not among them. My kids have always displayed an inability to tell a lie, even when they know the truth might not, in some particular circumstance, set them free.

> **ME:** Maggie! Did you dump out the hot cocoa powder all over the floor?
>
> Maggie's face crumples in anticipation of what is to come.
>
> **MAGGIE:** Ye-essss . . . (wretched sobbing)

Even if they know a time-out is forthcoming, even in the days when Seamus or Maggie couldn't talk yet and there was therefore a younger sibling on whom various acts of mischief could be blamed without fear of contradiction, my children have always either said nothing or told the truth. (Except when I ask Maggie if she needs to poop, and she yells, "No! I all better!" while ducking, red-faced, behind the sofa. In that case, however, there is a primal urge at work.)

Until recently, I am not sure my kids even knew the possibility of lying existed, let alone that they might use it to their advantage. Little children, at least mine, are truthful to the point of pain, like when Connor regarded my outfit one morning about six months after Maggie was born and said, "You know, Mommy, it's funny. Because you don't have a baby in your tummy anymore, but in that shirt, you still look a little bit pregmint." It was a new shirt. I thought I looked pretty good in it. Since David loved life too well to ever express such an opinion, I was thankful, even as I dropped the shirt in the Goodwill bag, that I had several tiny truth-tellers in my home.

Then, one recent morning, I called down the hall to Seamus:

ME: Shea, did you brush your teeth?
SEAMUS: Yup.

I ducked into the kids' bathroom to wipe down the Colgate SpongeBob SquarePants Anticavity Fluoride Toothpaste for Children (Spongy Bubbly Fruit Flavor) that, in my son's wake, would trail unfailingly across the sink top and down into the bowl. But the sink was perfectly neat, and his toothbrush, usually gummed up with unrinsed turquoise sludge, was completely dry. I went back down the hall and found Seamus playing calmly in his room, arranging his stuffed animal companions on his bed.

ME: Seamus, are you sure you brushed your teeth?
SEAMUS: Yup.
ME: Honey, I *know* that you didn't.

He looked up, surprised.

SEAMUS: Why? Were you wooking?

I told him that yes, the eyes in the back of my head could also see through bathroom doors, actually, and that was what had tipped me off. Seamus decided to test these powers by going back down the hall to the bathroom, closing the door, and asking if I could see the toothbrush in his mouth. Since he said it like this—"Maah eee, oo ee uh oo uss ih eye ow?"— I could say, with confidence, that of course I did, and I could tell through the door he was quite impressed.

Connor sometimes asks me if I really, for pinky swear, have eyes in the back of my head, and I tell him that I must, since I can always see everything he is doing behind me. This neat bit of motherly guile has probably been what has kept my children on the level: since they wouldn't be able to get anything over on me anyhow, they might as well tell the truth. But it occurs to me now that my children's belief in my mommy superpowers has come at the expense of my own honesty. In perpetuating the old Mom Eyes canard, I have lied to my children in order to keep them from lying to me. It seems only fit that such a parenting tactic might one day come back to bite me on the ass. Perhaps it already has.

Connor overheard me talking to David about his brother's bald-faced toothbrushing prevarication later that night and, as the eldest, felt obliged to put in his two cents:

CONNOR: Mommy, let me just tell you one thing. If you wonder if Seamus is telling a lie, don't wonder. Because he lies *all the time*.

He was being a tattletale, but I couldn't resist, because frankly this was news to me.

ME: What does he lie about, Connor?
CONNOR: Well. Every time he says I hit him? It's a lie.

Clearly, Connor was himself turning out to be an unreliable source.

Then, the following evening, Exhibit B. Connor had not seen bathwater in an embarrassing number of days, so I shooed him off to the shower while feeding his sister dinner. Ten minutes later, he emerged, towel around waist.

CONNOR: I took my shower, Mommy!

He was completely dry, except for his hair, which had a few wet spots on top, apparently added in haste from the bathroom sink.

ME: No, you didn't.
CONNOR: Yes I did, Mommy! Look, *my hair is wet*.
ME: Your hair is, like, one percent wet. I don't think you can *take* a shower and have your hair get only that wet.

Connor's eyes darted around as he searched for a backup story.

ME: Are you lying to me, Connor?

Connor sighed and turned back toward the bathroom.

CONNOR: Ohhh-kayyy. *Fiiinnne.*

Just how long had this been going on? I had been letting Connor shower without my supervision for several months, thrilled that the next time I saw him he would be squeaky clean and already in his pajamas. It seemed like the payoff I deserved for the three months of his babyhood when the mere sound of running bathwater made him weep. Now, I had to wonder just how long he and his brother had been opting out of their bathroom routines. Had Connor been wetting his head under the sink for months? Was the rest of him as filthy as I suddenly suspected?

Once you know your kids are lying to you about anything, you have to question what else they've been getting away with, and for how long. I was forced to reconsider all the "accidental" destructions of property I had let slide, like the time Seamus assured me that he didn't mean to groove deep scratches in the kitchen table with his Hess collectible cement truck, but it "zust happened." I began distrusting everything my children said:

SEAMUS: I bwushed my teef, Mommy.
ME: No you didn't. You weren't in there long enough.
SEAMUS: *Mom! I weawy did!*

And then I checked the toothbrush, and it *was* wet, and then I freaked out because by accusing him of lying when he wasn't even doing it, I was just putting it in his head to do it more, not exactly a concept I wanted to encourage.

My children are not supposed to lie to me! At least, not when they are one, four, and six years old. It is I who am supposed to lie to them! About the Easter Bunny, and the Tooth Fairy, and my utter certainty there will be absolutely no spiders in the basement the next time we go down there. Had they learned dishonesty from me? If so, I was surely to blame, although a parent lies to a child merely to preserve his innocence, to protect him from the world. Are not a parent's lies merely customary and sort of adorable? On the other hand, how can you tell your child that lying is bad after it has begun to dawn on him that Mommy has been telling whoppers of her own?

Here, I fear, is where my current troubles have begun. There is a stinky sock in every laundry basket, and in Connor's kindergarten class it is a kid named Jacob, who has an older brother in fifth grade named Leo. Leo is an even stinkier sock, the sort of stocky, thatch-haired kid you can easily imagine growing into his future destructive abilities, and having him for an older brother means Jacob is therefore treated by the other kindergartners with the great deference he deserves. Leo's words, as handed down by Jacob, are life, and so I should not have been as shocked as I was to hear Connor announce at the breakfast table one recent morning, "Jacob says that Leo says there's no such thing as Santa."

I froze, jelly knife in hand. Seamus froze, spoonful of eggs halfway to his mouth. Connor continued eating his Raisin Bran, watching me out of the corner of his eye.

I am going to brain that freaking Leo, was my first thought. Connor was too young to lose Santa, let alone four-year-old

Seamus, who had the misfortune to be the innocent younger brother of a kid who had a friend who had a creep of an older brother. It seemed to me, standing there with the jelly knife, that as long as children tell parents the truth *always,* and parents lie to their children *sometimes,* all is well. But when parents are forced to tell the truth to their children—which is, in the case of Santa Claus at least, that they have been putting their children on all their little lives—things start going off the rails. Once my children lost Santa, once they knew they could no longer believe everything I told them, some part of their childhood would be irretrievably lost as well. I had to think fast.

> **ME:** Well. In that case, I feel sorry for Leo.
> **CONNOR:** Why?
> **ME:** Because Santa only comes to the houses of people who believe in him. If you say you don't believe, you don't get toys.
> **CONNOR:** But Leo says your parents are the ones who really give you the toys.
> **ME:** At *his* house! Sure! Because Santa doesn't come to their house.
> **SEAMUS:** (just getting it) Santa *doesn't come* to dere house?
> **ME:** Isn't that sad? But Santa comes to *our* house, because you put out your stockings. And you believe. Right?
> **SEAMUS:** I bewieve in Santa, mmm-hmm.
> **CONNOR:** Me too! I believe too!

Seamus returned to his scrambled eggs, quite reassured. Connor, on the other hand, was working so hard to re-believe that his eyes were screwed shut, like Shirley Temple wishing her daddy back to life in *The Little Princess*. Since Connor wanted so deeply to accept my explanation, I think Santa is safe in our house for now. But it is hard to tell, since the closed circle of my logic—that you have to believe in Santa in order to get presents from him—means that Connor would probably never confess to being beyond it all even if he were, if there was a chance it meant an empty stocking on Christmas morn. Just in case Santa is real, he had better keep the faith, or at least act as if he still has it.

Now, in Connor's head, Santa has become inextricably linked with God, another larger-than-life character with wobbly backstory to which one must claim credence or risk the consequences. Since the dawn of religion, the justifications for God's existence have actually had some similarity to my Santa cover-up: you have to believe, or else. Faith in God is predicated upon believing in something no one has seen, and going to parochial school, I learned every day that good people believe in God, that one must believe in God to be good, and that good things happen to people who really, really believe in God. Now, when we are in church, Connor takes no chances: he praises the Lord at top volume. "God is real, just like Santa is real!" he announced the last time we were leaving Mass, shocking several of the old ladies saying the rosary in the front pews with this bit of blasphemy. "Yeah, and God even *wooks wike* Santa!" Seamus chimed in, and he had a point there. But it's more than the long white beards linking these two affable and possibly fictional old men in my children's heads. They know that they are supposed to believe in Santa and in God, and so they will continue to at least claim to do so, even when, in their heads, it may make no sense.

I remember figuring out that Santa was a sham when

I was six. I read it somewhere, in some book that had yet another snotty older sibling shattering the illusions of the elementary-school protagonist. I never needed to ask my mother if it was true—there it was, in print—but neither was I saddened by my loss of innocence. I felt that I had entered the adult world, an entirely separate sphere where there were many things understood of which mere children knew nothing. I wanted to signal my coming of age to my college-aged aunts and uncles at our Christmas Eve party that year, especially Uncle Marty, who always made everyone laugh but whose jokes usually went over my head. I wanted to show Uncle Marty that from now on, I was one of the cognoscenti, ready to learn the secret handshake. I drew him a picture of a bug-eyed owl saying, "Santa Claus: WHOOOO is this man?" Uncle Marty looked at it. "Uh, okay there, Ame," he said, and then my father took it away and said if I didn't stop drawing stuff like that with the little cousins around I was going to get in big trouble. Even though my owl drawing was subtle to the point of inscrutability, I was not supposed to teach children younger than me to question in any way the fictions that they—and their parents—held so dear.

Even that rebuke did not dampen my enthusiasm for the exhilarating World of Lies I had entered. I was thrilled to have crossed over, to have become part of the side that kept the secrets rather than the side to whom it had never occurred that there *were* any. Up until then, I had not really understood that deception, even benign deception, was possible. Now I knew I could lie to my parents about all sorts of things, although most of what I kept from them was innocent enough that I probably should not have gone to the trouble.

At the end of my freshman year of high school, I suffered

my first romantic breakup, losing my boyfriend to an older woman: a senior. The glamour of their age difference dazzled Doug, blinding him to the inescapable fact that Sharon was kind of a loser. I mean, she was in the wind ensemble. Still, she stole Doug from me without any wavering on his part, and I was informed by a personal note from Sharon, delivered via a mutual acquaintance. "You stay away from Doug or else YOUR ASS IS GRASS!!" Sharon concluded, with lots of underlines. I went home to my room that afternoon and attempted to burn this letter, along with all the notes Doug had ever passed me in algebra during our five-month romance. After a few tries I gave up; the paper sort of smoldered rather than leaping into flame, and the cathartic effects were not what I had hoped. Even so, my mother knocked on the door ten minutes later. I opened it, my face a mask of irreproachability.

MY MOTHER: What's that smell?
ME: What smell?
MY MOTHER: Like something burning.
ME: I don't smell anything.
MY MOTHER: Well, I do, and it's coming from your room.
ME: No, see, my window's open, so it's coming from outside. Maybe our neighbors were burning something.

I remember seeing clearly on my mother's face that (1) she did not believe me, but (2) she was not exactly sure what it was she was accusing me of. So she left. Maybe she thought I was experimenting with cigarettes, and I probably should have just owned up to what I was really doing, which was a good deal less transgressive. By this point, though, I had stopped telling my mother pretty much anything, so she had no idea that Doug had broken up with me. She may not have even been aware, come to think of it, of who Doug even was. To have to start from the beginning and explain his existence, and that now I might have to fight a senior who was saying that my ass was grass, was unthinkable. I lied and called it "nothing," simply because it was too exhausting to lay it all out.

I wonder now why I was so certain my mother could not have understood how I was feeling, why I had to keep the details of my first heartbreak from her rather than break down and cry on her shoulder. But my first instinct was not to tell her everything; it was to save myself the trouble. This is how, I think, the split between a child and her mother begins. It is less about cunning falsehoods than about little lies of omission, things left out that are not worth expressing, that grow slowly but surely until what you do not share with your mother dwarfs what you do, in a distracted and once-weekly phone call.

In an attempt to keep our family lines of communication more open than this with my own children, I have established a dinnertime tradition over the last couple of years. Each evening, after I heap second helpings of macaroni and cheese on the kids' plates, I sit down (finally) at the table with them and ask them to give me a show of thumbs on how their days were. We have greatly improved on the original Siskel and Ebert system, because in our ratings methodology, each thumb can go up, middle, or down, perhaps even independently of the other, creating six possible levels of satisfaction on our sliding scale. After giving their daily rating, everyone can elaborate on the reasons for a classification, telling the rest of the family what made it, say, a middle thumb/down thumb combo day.

Connor used to beg to go first. Now he doesn't want to play at all. "IIucch, I don't want to *talk about it,*" he says, and I can see that it's a mild irritation, that there's not some deep dark secret he's keeping, it's just that none of the kindergarten intrigue seems worth mentioning. Then the next day, his science teacher will see me at drop-off and say, "Did Connor tell you about the chicken we dissected? He got right in there!" and I can't believe he didn't race home from Kindergarten M to tell me. He dissected a *chicken*? That's a hell of a lot more interesting than anything that happened to me in kindergarten. (Or *this* year, for that matter.) I can't help but feel hurt that at six, he is already excluding me from his inner life. But when I was his age, I was similarly certain that the details of my own school day required so much color commentary that they were not worth getting into. Besides, my mother wouldn't understand any of it anyway. She didn't *really* want to know, and if I kept not telling her, maybe she'd stop asking. Now I am my mother, hungering for details of the majority of each day Connor spends without me and getting nothing.

It is strange to realize that Connor has entire days' worth of experiences he doesn't tell me about, of which I am completely unaware, and that this is how it will be, more and more, from now on. I lied to Connor to protect him from the world, and someday, he will lie to protect his world from me. I hope that he will tell me when his first girlfriend dumps him, rather than suffer in silence, because kissing boo-boos is what a mother is for. But he may well not, and someday there might even be things he keeps from me not because they are too draining to discuss but because he knows it is his mother's innocence that needs to be protected.

Seamus, at least, still plays the dinnertime thumb game with great gusto:

Seamus: My day was bad? 'Cause it was waining.
And it was gweat? 'Cause it was hot dogs for wunch.

He is nothing if not succinct, but these brief summations are to him the most important details he could wish to share. He is too young to want to hide anything from me. At least I hope so.

Sometimes Seamus has a hard time falling asleep at night and will sneak back out to the living room long after David and I assume all of our children are dead to the world. When he staggers into the living room, jammies askew, squinting at the light coming from the television, we usually lead him back to his bed pretty quickly. But one night recently I let him lie with me for a few amicable minutes, holding him tight as David flipped through the channels. When David looked over at us from his side of the couch, he was moved by this picture of domestic devotion.

David: Seamus, don't you have the best mommy?

Seamus thought about it for a moment.

Seamus: No.
Me: Excuse me?
Seamus: No. You are not de *best* mommy. In anudder house, there is pwobby a mommy who is gooder.

DAVID: Seamus, that's not nice to say.
SEAMUS: But it's twue. You still a good mommy.
You're zust not the *best* mommy.

He snuggled back into my chest, quite contented.

What could I say? He was so obviously, totally right.
Even if his candor was tough love, I could also see it as a precious resource, a dying light. As long as Seamus still told me
the honest truth, and as long as I could still tell him stories
to keep him safe, he would still be a child. So I squeezed
Seamus tighter, smiling even at his conjuring of some other,
gooder mommy, because at least it meant he was still, for a
little while longer, fully mine.

CHAPTER TWENTY

Unaccompanied Mother

One Sunday evening last fall, David was in our bedroom packing for a weeklong business trip to Los Angeles while I was in
the kitchen feeding the three kids their dinner. They all had
their peas and carrots, they all had their cups of milk, and
all three of them were eating. Happily. It was one of those
strange and rare moments when I had, for just a moment,
nothing in particular to do. My cell phone was sitting there on
the counter, and when I picked it up, I saw a voice mail message from early that morning that I had not, until then, had
time to notice. I pressed play and held it to my ear to listen.

"Amy, I have to leave the country," my then-babysitter
Jenny said in her plummy British accent, though her voice
sounded small, and distant, and not really like her. "My mum
is sick and I'm on the next flight home to London. I don't
know how long I'll be gone, I don't know what to tell you, I
have to go." Click.

Jenny had been our babysitter for only three months. She
was Mary Poppins come to life. I kept telling David she was too

good to be true. (Since we would never see her again, it appears I was right about that.) I put down the phone, watching my three children eat their wagon-wheel pasta with their fingers— Connor was five then, Seamus four, Maggie barely a year—and while I was concerned for poor Jenny, I was more concerned about how the hell I was going to get through the next week.

I am often alone with all three kids. Because David works twelve-hour days, I handle getting all three kids up, fed, dressed, and out the door in the mornings, and most of the time, I am the one ushering them through *Max and Ruby*, teeth brushing, and edifying bedtime stories on the downslide to nighty-night. But this is not *really* alone. Rare is the full day and night where there is neither husband nor babysitter nor weekend birthday party to keep some percentage of my children out of my hair for a couple of hours. Now the celestial bodies had aligned David's travel, Jenny's unexpected absence, and the preschool fall break just so, creating an eclipse of six days' duration where I would be on my own with my children.

I was a little panicked by the prospect of that much solo parenting. I could also see that was kind of pathetic. This was something any mother worth her salt should be able to handle. My mother managed all six of us when my CPA dad went underground for tax season. My grandmother herded eight without breaking stride. If I went ahead and had three children, I should be able to handle them all on my own for a week, right? If only to get back in touch with my masochistic side? "Just accept you won't get anything else done," David advised me as he packed his socks. It was good advice. For the foreseeable future, I would not write, or check my e-mail, or apply moisturizer, or sit down. I would be on duty.

After David left for the airport on Monday morning I gave the kids a calm and loving speech on how there were three kids but only one mommy, and how everyone was going to have to step up his or her game. Maggie just stared at me, gumming her frozen bagel in her high chair, but she showed uncharacteristic nap flexibility with the boys' school pickups and drop-offs. Seamus had to miss his gym class because Maggie napped then instead. Connor followed through on his pledge to be my Big Boy Who Would Not Whine. All three of them, I must say, were troupers.

And yet, it was I who was *great*. By telling myself I was in an extended sort of X Games Mothering Competition, I managed to get through the first five days without becoming Bold Mommy even once. I made eye contact and spoke in a low, firm voice, even when all three children were crying at the same time. I breathed deeply while Connor sobbed, fifteen minutes past bedtime, about how "not tired" he was. I remained calm when Seamus covered his palms with a uniform coat of his orange poop, like a pore-tightening clay mask. I even kept it together when Maggie crawled in the shower with me at 5:45 A.M. with my makeup bag in her hand, and dumped all its contents out in the running water. I felt that my execution had been flawless. On the wave of this rather excessive self-confidence, I decided to finish my unforgettable performance with a double axel/triple Salchow combination sure to catch the eyes of the mothering judges: I would fly to Florida for a long weekend with all three children, unaccompanied by any other set of capable hands.

Admittedly, this ultimate challenge had been thrust upon me. Our tickets had been purchased long ago, David had always planned to meet us there, and Jenny, who was supposed to travel with me and the kids, was not returning my increasingly urgent text messages. But after how I had performed all week, I felt ready. I had actually flown solo with the kids once before, and survived, and had been amazed by the attention we received along the way. "Oh, sweetheart, you have the best mother I have ever *seen!*" the TSA agent had said, chucking baby Maggie under the chin before returning to her usual surly self with the passengers behind us. As my ducklings and I deplaned in Florida, the pilot was so impressed by the boys' behavior that he let them stick around to see the cockpit.

It was one of the few times I have felt my hard work as a mother was actually seen and appreciated. Fathers receive adulation like this all the time. If David has more than one of our children under his care for more than three minutes, people line up to tell him what an incredible father he is, even if I'm only in the restroom. But mothers hardly ever get this kind of attention for doing what is considered to be merely our job. After all, if we are good mothers, it's not even supposed to be hard for us. But flying alone with three children? That gets a mother noticed, and so I was looking forward to this day of travel just a tiny bit. After the week I had had, I deserved a pat on the back.

I was humming as I strapped the children into their car seats at 7:15 A.M. the next morning, before zooming off to the airport with the following items carefully organized in our carry-ons:

- six diapers
- four bottles
- a change of clothes for Maggie
- sweatshirts in case the plane was cold

- blankies for all three children
- a dizzying array of nut-free sandwiches and snacks
- Ziploc bags and plastic shopping bags (for diaper messes and end-of-flight trash organization)
- DVD player (in case the in-flight TV malfunctioned)
- backup battery (in case the DVD battery malfunctioned)
- an entire Velcro'd sleeve of age-appropriate DVD viewing options
- four sets of headphones
- paper
- crayons
- stickers
- books my kids hadn't seen before
- and my secret ingredient: an ongoing collection of the crap my kids get in party favor bags and at fast-food restaurants, saved carefully for just such an occasion.

We had enough supplies to last a fortnight's delay on the tarmac. Even if I would need almost none of it, experience had taught me that preparation is the best prevention. Packing these bags was my finest hour.

When we went through the security checkpoint, I had to remove everyone's shoes, including Maggie's tiny Robeez, which are soft baby shoes for babies who do not walk yet and that do not, strictly speaking, *have* soles in which a terrorist might hide an explosive device. But I digress. I left my new jacket behind at the X-ray machine but kept track of all three kids! As I strolled to the gate with Maggie in her sling, pulling our carry-ons behind me and over both shoulders, my sons walking calmly alongside me holding on to my belt loops, I drank in the admiring stares of the travelers going the other way on the people mover, and I thought, *Damn. I* am *good at this.*

We waited until the last minute to board the plane, because contrary to popular opinion, I think that people traveling with small children should be the *last* to board the tiny metal flying box from which there is no escape. The boys stayed pressed to the plate-glass window counting the duffel bags entering the cargo hold until final boarding call. I was pacing with Maggie, who was very fussy and kept refusing her bottle. But then again, it was past her nap time. As we boarded the plane together, I saw the panic in the eyes of those passengers seated near seats 4A, 4B, and 4C. *These people don't know me,* I was thinking, *or my kids. When we land, they're going to stop by our row just to tell me how unbelievably well-behaved my children were.* After all, that was what had happened the last time.

Plus, now that we were aboard the plane, the hardest part was over. Connor and Seamus would not be heard from again once I adjusted their headphones, because we were flying JetBlue, which streams the wonders of Cartoon Network and Nickelodeon directly to the seats of children lucky enough to fly their jocular skies. Three or more hours of cartoon viewing, interrupted only by a nice lady inquiring whether they would like chocolate-chip biscotti or Doritos Snack Mix? This was Elysium for any lad. All I had to do was coax Maggie down for her nap, and then there was a leftover *Us Weekly* in the seat-back pocket calling my name.

By now Maggie was way overdue for her nap; she cried all through takeoff and would not take her bottle, no matter how many times I proffered it. She was still whimpering by the time the seat belt sign went off, so I got out of my seat to stroll up and down the aisle with her in the sling, certain this was all she would need to nod off. I jostled her up and down, which she usually enjoyed. "Huuuhhh," Maggie cried gutturally, and as we approached the front of the plane, she let loose a torrent of vomit, washing over her, me, and the sling that bound us together.

The two flight attendants, still chatting in their jump seats, looked at us, jaws agape. "Oh my *God*," one said in a low voice. As Maggie continued vomiting, I stepped calmly, calmly, into the tiny bathroom, as if I had known this was going to happen; looked at myself in the mirror; and said, "Keep it together."

I wet a wad of paper towels and cleaned the both of us off as best I could, then returned to our seats, where I pulled out Maggie's spare outfit *and* spare sling. I changed her and put the smelly clothes in one of the Ziploc bags. Since I had left my jacket behind at the security checkpoint, I turned my sweater inside out so the throw-up stains wouldn't be as obvious. And the boys, although I had to climb right over them to do all this, never even looked up from SpongeBob.

I sat there thinking, *My God, I just handled this. And it wasn't even that big a deal! I am the Mother of the Year!* Then Maggie looked up at me, retched, and cascaded a fresh supply of throw-up all over both of us, the seat-back table, and everything I had just changed her into.

Now we were attracting some attention. The woman in 3A turned and peered at me through the crack in the seat accusingly, as if I were somehow causing this horror. *Why is this lady letting her baby throw up right behind me?* she was clearly thinking. *Just stick her in the overhead compartment!* Maggie looked up at me, sweaty and jaundiced, also wondering just why I didn't do something about this. The flight attendants, who could *see* me (in row 4) from where they were sitting, looked aghast at both of us but just sat there. I had to ring the call button in order for one of them to approach, with her scarf over her face.

"Can I, um, have some paper towels or something?" I said.

She just stared at both of us.

"I'd, uh, get them myself, but I have a puddle of vomit on my lap," I added helpfully.

She came back, threw a pile of gray single-ply napkins at me, performed a Lysol-spraying vogue in the aisle, and beat a hasty retreat back to the front of the plane.

Now, imagine this whole thing happening *four more times*.

Please consider, if you will: I was flying to Orlando. Some flights on that corridor probably have a 1:1 child-to-adult ratio. If, even once a year, one child on one flight vomits everywhere, because babies do not *know* they are about to throw up, nor that they should ask their mothers to retrieve the airsick bag intended for such moments, the airline might want to have something more substantial than the tiny bits of scratchy, reconstituted wood pulp they provide with our miniature cans of apple juice on offer as a cleaning device. There wasn't even a roll of Bounty aboard, let alone some Ajax and a sponge. The flight attendants weren't about to clean it up, they were making that eminently clear, but I would have been glad to, had I had something to do it with. Instead, I had only a meager pile of generic-brand facial tissue with which to battle the onslaught of Maggie's puke, which geysered anew every twenty minutes or so.

The flight attendants were exactly zero help. Obviously they resented Maggie for stinking up the whole plane and me for not bringing my own disinfectant, mop, and bucket aboard, but the disgusted stares they aimed at me from their jump seats for the duration of the flight seemed a bit much. There were, I thank the Lord, two angels on board. The lady across the aisle, who had been enjoying two empty seats (one of them Jenny's) next to her, invited Connor and Seamus over to her side so that they might not be covered in vomit as well. She even put their headphones back on so that their *Krypto the Superdog* coma could continue unabated (although Connor did look up once, during the transfer, and ask, "What is that *smell*?"). This lady didn't ask me before moving the boys, she just did it, and I was so grateful I wanted to hug her, although I am not sure she would have been receptive to that in my current state. There was also the man behind us, who in between Maggie's vomiting sessions tried to ease her misery by valiantly jingling his change. But Maggie would have none of it. When she was not retching, she could only sob, damp with sweat. (It would be two days or so before I would deduce that Maggie was suffering from rotavirus, which is brought on by contact with fecal matter. Seamus and his self-administered poop paraffin treatment? *J'accuse*.)

When we at last arrived in Florida, everyone stayed in their seats to let our family off first. This was less an act of chivalry than of self-preservation. The flight attendants looked pointedly away, eyes rolled heavenward and hands over noses as we passed. Maggie celebrated our arrival in the gate area by yakking again, then once more as we rode the monorail to baggage claim. By this point I had abandoned all cleanup attempts: we both had barf on our shirts, in our hair, on our pants. I even had it on my shoes. Maggie was too weak to cry anymore; she would sort of mew, hanging there in her vomity sling, and then let it rip. As we rode the monorail, with me and her and the boys on one end and sixty-five other travelers sardined at the other, no one hailed my mothering skills. No one was even making eye contact. *Thank God,* each one of them was thinking, *that I am not her.* And I certainly agreed with them—at that moment, one should have wanted to be anyone in the world but me. I was not the Mother of the Year. I was Sissy Spacek in *Carrie,* untouchable, covered in gore, leaving behind the scorched earth of her senior prom. All I could do was keep looking straight ahead, heading for the exit.

Perhaps, I thought to myself, I had deserved those flight attendants' scorn. What kind of mother would fly with a sick baby? Why hadn't I brought along eight extra outfits instead of just one? In my hubris, I had thought I was ready for every conceivable thing that could happen on that plane, and I was still left unprepared. But holding on to that monorail pole, I realized: being a mother is like that. Again and again, motherhood will throw at me things for which I will feel, and may indeed be, completely unprepared. What will decide whether or not I am a good mother is not whether I am ready for such times, but how I move through the door.

Once the monorail came to its complete stop, I exited with my head held high, Maggie strapped to me, Seamus by the hand, Connor on the other side helping me drag our belongings. I was not the picture of a mother failing. I was a mother valiantly succeeding despite all that had happened. We were not home free yet: we were off to stand in line at the car rental counter before I strapped them in for another ninety-minute ride, along an interstate where I could only hope there might be a Target to purchase some Pedialyte and some new clothes, and perhaps a McDonald's for two starving boys. But somehow or other, I would find a way. I was a pioneer woman, going boldly where no nonparent would go. In that moment, I was fearless. *That's right,* I thought, taking in the stares at baggage claim with pride. *I survived.*

CHAPTER TWENTY-ONE

But Yes the Mommy

This summer, Maggie has become old enough to express vehement preference on what her bedtime story should be each evening, and whatever story she chooses from the pile, I can be certain it will be from the canon of Sandra Boynton. Ms. Boynton's deceptively simple board books (suitable for chewing by their very youngest readers) feature an array of cartoon animals with wide-eyed, serious expressions, going matter-of-factly about the business of, say, donning pajamas, or square dancing. Maggie is as obsessed with Boynton's books as both of her older brothers were at her age. This may be because I force-fed them down all three of their little throats, but how could I not? I find Boynton's books some of the most appealingly drawn, humorously written, and sneakily thought-provoking literature out there, and I am including books for grown-ups in that equation.

My own favorite Sandra Boynton book is *But Not the Hippopotamus,* the tale of a young semiaquatic mammal who is not keeping pace with her animal companions:

A cat and two rats
Are trying on hats.
But not the hippopotamus.
A moose and a goose
Together have juice.
But not the hippopotamus.

The hippopotamus watches all these gay activities peeking from behind a tree, or from the corner table where she sits alone, or through the window of a haberdashery (literally, on the outside looking in). The other animals aren't excluding her intentionally; they don't even know she's there, which is ironic, because she is certainly the largest animal in the book. The hippo's face is a perfect, childish blank of huge-eyed concern. She desperately wants to be included in all the fun but is just not sure how to make her move. All the other animals run past the hippopotamus, out for a group jog in their new hats, while she gazes after them longingly. But just when they all appear to have left the hippo behind, Boynton throws us a curveball:

But then the pack
Comes scurrying back
Saying, Hey! Come join the lot of us!
And she just doesn't know:
Should she stay? Should she go?

Caught up in her indecision, the hippo's front hooves hover near her face in a way I find nearly heartbreaking. Turn the page, though, and she runs after her friends, suddenly weightless, absolutely free, calling,

But YES the hippopotamus!

I always find it thrilling when the hippopotamus casts off her uncertainty and runs off to play. It is when she feels free to join in on the fun that she comes alive and looks, finally, happy. I want that joyful ending for the little hippo, because I know well what it is like to hang back. I too will hide behind a tree if I fear I cannot do something perfectly.

Every Friday of second grade, I told my mother I had a stomachache in a vain attempt to miss gym class, taught by the dreaded Mrs. Backus, a gravelly-voiced, deeply tanned senior citizen with no patience for the hesitant. I hated the ignominy of sides-choosing, in which I was inevitably second-to-last, ahead only of the boy who still wet his pants. I hated the queasy feeling I got when Mrs. Backus got out the red kickball and announced we were, once again, playing Kill the Guy. I hated standing at the free-point line to miss another basket with everyone watching. I hated the pressure of performing something I would never be any good at.

Now that I'm an adult, I continue to be terrified of any arena where my meager athletic skills might be exposed, such as a family reunion softball game. I have no idea how to exist in that world. I am still not sure on which hand one wears a baseball mitt. And I will probably never learn, since if I can't immediately be good at something I hang back and watch instead. My hesitation extends beyond sports, however. Even if it's just a pack of preschool moms meeting up for a coffee, even if I really want to participate, I still wait to be asked. While the moms of other toddlers chat easily at the playground, trading phone numbers as we all stand around, I want to say, "Can Maggie and I come over tomorrow too? See, she's my third, I am lazy, and she has no friends." We're all grown-ups; what are they going to say, no? That should be easy for me to say by now. But I say nothing.

This is how I am. But I wish I were not. When I read *But Not the Hippopotamus,* I always root for the hippo to overcome her shyness. I want my kids to understand that they do not have to miss out on their own lives, stuck in their own moments of self-doubt.

Each July, the kids and I leave the city and move a hundred miles away until Labor Day. It is the escape valve that makes life in New York City feel possible. When we are out here, the kids can lie in the grass and pick dandelions and enjoy a slower pace of life. On Saturday mornings, David and I take the kids to the local baseball field for a pickup game. This is no hyper-organized Little League but a very gentle and encouraging game, where the kids are on one eternal batting team and a couple of dads do the pitching and fielding. The dads time their plays carefully so that no one is ever tagged out, and everyone at bat gets to swing until they hit. Maggie and I sit in the grass and watch as David and the boys dash to the far side of the fence with their gloves. I like to imagine, watching them, that things might have turned out differently for me if I went to a game like this when I was their age.

Even so, Seamus will usually take only a few half-assed turns at bat before walking around the fence to sit on my lap in the grass. Last week, he rolled his eyes back until the whites showed, so that he would not cry. "I not vewy good at baseball," he whispered.

"But you are, honey! You hit the ball so many times!" I

cooed, smoothing his hair. It didn't work. He was done for the day. As someone whom sports always made cry, I let him stay there in my lap, even though David was a little annoyed. But my son's disappointment killed me, because for someone who was not quite five, he was doing just fine. It was only his own diffidence that was keeping Seamus from cracking the ball as confidently as he did in our own backyard. All he needed to do was go back out there, and have fun, and not give a rat's ass whether he was any good or not. But I could not explain how to do that.

My other two children are not like me in this way. Maggie runs at life full speed and hugs it about the knees. As soon as she is old enough to take the field—and probably well before—she will be right out there, slugging with the big kids. Connor, too, is able to embrace new opportunities eagerly. This summer, he attended a new day camp and got on a school bus by himself for the very first time. Since his first day of camp was two weeks after the other kids had started, I fretted that all alliances would have been made already, permanently excluding him. "How do you feel?" I asked him as we stood at the end of the driveway.

"A little nervous. 'Cause it's my first day. But I'll be okay," he answered calmly, boarding the school bus without a tear or a look back. "My son doesn't know *anyone*," I told the bus driver, sotto voce. "Please make sure he finds his way." The bus driver nodded with a slight roll of the eyes; he had evidently seen mothers like me before. He knew that Connor would be fine. So did Connor. I, however, was not so sure, and is it not a mother's prerogative to hover?

When I dropped Seamus off at his younger, gentler day camp that same morning (no school bus yet for him), I leaned on the college-aged counselors. You have to engage him in activities with his peers, I told them. Otherwise he will just sit there. I wanted them to understand: Seamus needed help to get past his innate bashfulness to where the other children were. The counselors looked at Seamus, then at me, a little confused, since he seemed perfectly happy in the corner doing a puzzle and humming to himself. They were not as invested as I was in seeing Seamus run outside with the other children, laughing and shouting. I was the only one worried about what he will miss this summer if he stays inside, waiting for someone to ask him if he wouldn't like a turn on the swings.

But my children have to negotiate their camp experiences for themselves. That is the point of going. Their mother is supposed to be absent, just as there is no mother hippopotamus present in the pages of Boynton's book to nudge her little hippo along. Maybe there is nothing the mama hippo could say or do that would really help, anyway. The little hippopotamus has to come out from behind the tree herself, and Seamus will have to learn on his own to say "hello" back to that nice little boy who wants to play with him. But even if Seamus finds the nerve to join the pack, I will still be lurking behind that tree, watching, biting my fingernails.

It occurs to me that this hovering in the background, worrying, not knowing what I'm supposed to do, is how I feel—as a mother—most of the time. I watch my children as they venture away from me, praying that their lives will be easy and carefree. But I cannot fret away the inevitable bumps in their roads, and my presence cannot really change, at those times, whether they are going to feel like the little hippopotamus or not.

But the background is where a mother belongs, in bad and good times both. I am supposed to be the responsible adult at all times, standing back and watching the fun, ready to interrupt if things get too silly or dangerous. Mothers can't take part in the merrymaking because they are too busy enabling it behind the scenes. I used to think my mother never wore a bathing suit in the summer because she just didn't like swimming, or something. Now I see that it's because she never got around to putting it on. On a summer Saturday afternoon, David and the kids go jump in the pool after lunch. "I'll be right there!" I yell after them. But by the time I clean up the kitchen, and throw a load of clothes in the dryer, and go out to the pool, and pick up the towels thrown around, and then go back to the kitchen to get drinks for everyone, and then distribute the juice boxes, everyone is out of the pool, and I will have missed the fun again.

David does not have to be the juice box manager or bedtime clock watcher. His main job, when he is with the kids, is to be Good-Time Charlie, and to push the boundaries of what our children think they can do. If I say, "Be careful on those monkey bars," David is next to me saying, "Let me see how high you can climb." This past winter, David took Connor skiing a couple of times. (I have never skied in my life.) David told Seamus he would be old enough to go along with them next year. "Maybe Mommy will come too," David said, winking at me. "You and Mommy can learn to ski together." Since this would be an acceptable excuse for a grown woman to be on the bunny slope, I agreed I would give it a shot. Then Natasha Richardson's tragic death, the result of a seemingly minor bump on the head during a ski lesson, occurred just a week later. "Well, that's it," I told David. "Two little boys without a mother? You'll never get me on skis now." He, choosing his arguments like any good husband does, has not pushed me any further. But when he heads out to the slope with our boys next winter—and even Maggie, in a few more years—and I stay home, what will that cost? What will Maggie learn from watching her mother always sitting on the sidelines? What will I miss while I wait for them all to return safely to the bottom of the mountain?

But Not the Hippopotamus does not really end with the hippo's joining in the fun. There is an afterword of sorts, one that I have always found a bit thorny. As the hippopotamus runs off to play, she shouts,

But YES the hippopotamus!

And then, looking after her forlornly, is another uncertain young mammal:

But not the armadillo.

The armadillo, drawn with shaky lines, is fraught with uncertainty. (The hippopotamus had it easy compared to him.) The book ends without telling us whether the armadillo ever gets to join in, and I have always been sort of dissatisfied with this ending. Why didn't Boynton end on a high note, with the hippo's moment of triumph? Maybe Boynton wants to remind her young readers that there will always be someone watching from the sidelines, feeling excluded, feeling shy. Or perhaps that armadillo is there for mothers like me, to remind us that feeling left out is normal. That our children can feel that way and still be okay. That they might *need* to feel that way at some point, and then overcome it on their own, in order to grow up at all.

My children are still very young. As they grow, parenting will be more and more about letting go, about helping them learn to help themselves. My worrying about what lies in their futures will not, alone, prevent bad things from happening. Planning ahead of time for every possible consequence may just mean that I miss the thing that is really happening right now. There may be times when it is all right to risk imperfection, even failure, and just join in, before my children no longer want my participation at all. Being the hippopotamus, always in the background, is on its face good mothering, but that is not the mother I really want to be.

My youngest brother is visiting us this week. He is a generation younger than I am, still in college, the liminal space between carefree childhood and responsible adulthood. My kids regard him, rightly, as "a little bit big and a little bit little." He was splashing in the pool with the kids yesterday, and I went outside to say that it was time to get out so they could begin their evening bath/dinner/story/bedtime routine. "Aren't you coming in?" my brother says, holding Maggie as she splashes, not realizing I had barely been in the pool all summer. "Come on in, Mom!" Connor yells, his goggles making him look like a mad scientist. "Yeah, Mom!" Seamus hollers. "It's weawy nice in here!" And even though I just blow-dried my hair that morning, even though I should be back in the house starting dinner, even though I know the cold will be bracing, I cannonball in the deep end.

Acknowledgments

I am very grateful to all of the following people:

Tracy Fisher, the agent whose insight, expertise, and unswerving belief in me improved this book immeasurably (and to her assistant, Elizabeth Reed);

Laurie Chittenden, the editor whose enthusiasm and wisdom were daily gifts, and who made my first book a much easier labor than my first child;

Brian Liebman, who was the first person to suggest that there was a book here, and who was instrumental in making it happen;

Mollie Wilson, who was peppered with drafts and almost-daily editorial questions, and is the best "first reader" a sister could have;

Julie Kramer, Heather Brudz, AJ Murphy, and Isabel Rose, who also read early versions of this book and provided much-needed encouragement during the writing process;

Everyone at HarperCollins—Liate Stehlik, Peggy Hageman, Shelby Meizlik and Seale Ballenger, Kimberly Chocolaad, Lynn Grady, and Jean Marie Kelly, Mike Brennan and all the wonderful salespeople, Dale Rohrbaugh, Mary Schuck, Mary Ann Petyak, and Aja Pollock;

Gretchen Koss and Meghan Walker at Tandem Literary, who worked tirelessly on behalf of this book and made it fun;

The "Mums Who Write," for the been-there-done-that advice and subtitle inspiration;

Linda Davis, Shelly Holassie, Sarah Kennedy, Katie Knick, Michael Wilson, YaYa and Poppy, and Nana and Pop—the babysitting village without whom I could never have written at all;

Heather Brudz, Cece Heraty, and Nicole Smallwood, who generously allowed me to include their "when did I get like this?" moments along with my own.

Most of all, I am grateful to the four reasons I get out of bed every morning: Connor, Seamus, Maggie, and David. Thank you for loving me enough to share me with this book for almost a year. Now: let's go play.